MALCOLM X TALKS TO YOUNG PEOPLE

Speeches in the U.S., Britain, and Africa

PATHFINDER
New York London Montréal Sydney

Edited by Steve Clark

Copyright © 1965, 1970, 1991 by Betty Shabazz and Pathfinder Press

ISBN 0-87348-628-5 paper; ISBN 0-87348-631-5 cloth
Library of Congress Catalog Card No. 90-64197
Manufactured in the United States of America

First edition, 1991

Cover and book design by Toni Gorton

Cover portrait by Carole Byard, from the Pathfinder Mural in New York
City. Photo by Margrethe Siem.

017207
323.092

Pathfinder
410 West Street, New York, NY 10014, U.S.A.

Pathfinder distributors around the world:
Australia (and Asia and the Pacific):
  Pathfinder, 19 Terry St., Surry Hills, Sydney, NSW 2010
Britain (and Europe, Africa, and the Middle East):
  Pathfinder, 47 The Cut, London, SE1 8LL
Canada:
  Pathfinder, 6566, boul. St-Laurent, Montréal, Québec, H2S 3C6
Iceland:
  Pathfinder, Klapparstíg 26, 2d floor, 121 Reykjavík
New Zealand:
  Pathfinder, 157a Symonds Street, Auckland
Sweden:
  Pathfinder, Vikingagatan 10, S-113 42, Stockholm
United States (and Caribbean and Latin America):
  Pathfinder, 410 West Street, New York, NY 10014

Malcolm X Talks to Young People

CONTENTS

Preface 6

About the cover 8

"When you get into a conversation on racism and discrimination and segregation," Malcolm X observed in January 1965, "you will find young people more incensed over it—they feel more filled with an urge to eliminate it."

With this in mind, Malcolm X seized every occasion to talk with young people. "It is the teenagers abroad, all over the world, who are actually involving themselves in the struggle to eliminate oppression and exploitation," he said.

Five such discussions during the last year of Malcolm X's life are presented in this book.

These talks were given following Malcolm X's March 1964 break with the Nation of Islam. Malcolm X had already long been a revolutionary advocate of Black rights and an intransigent opponent of the U.S. government and its imperialist policies. During the final months of 1964 and early 1965 he expressed an increasingly anticapitalist and, then, prosocialist point of view as well.

The speeches and the interview in this collection reflect how his political outlook was evolving, a process still under way when he was assassinated in February 1965.

They also reflect the wide audience Malcolm X had won among young people on several continents. During the year before his death, he made two extensive trips to Africa and the Middle East and several short trips to Europe. Three of the five discussions in this collection took place in Africa and Britain.

During this period the influence of Malcolm X's ideas also spread to young fighters against segregation in the United States, such as the high school students from McComb, Mississippi, whom he met with at the beginning of 1965.

Most of the material in this book is printed here for the first time. That is the case with the speeches at Oxford

University and the London School of Economics, only a few paragraphs of which have previously been in print. Excerpts from the talk to the students from McComb appeared in the Pathfinder pamphlet previously published under the title *Malcolm X Talks to Young People*. The speeches in Oxford and London and to the McComb students have been transcribed by Pathfinder from audiotape.

The speech at the University of Ghana was transcribed from audiotape by Ed Smith. It first appeared in Smith's *Where To, Black Man? An American Negro's African Diary* (Chicago: Quadrangle, 1967) and has long been out of print.

Two other items in this book are taken from the pamphlet version of *Malcolm X Talks to Young People:* the interview Malcolm X gave in January 1965 to the *Young Socialist* magazine, and a tribute to him shortly following his death by Jack Barnes, then national chairman of the Young Socialist Alliance.

✦ ✦ ✦

Alice Windom, who helped organize events for Malcolm X during his May 1964 trip to Ghana, provided photographs and information on this visit. Additional information on this trip was supplied by Ed Smith. Pathfinder also appreciates the assistance provided by the staff of the Library of the Oxford Union Society and the British Library of Political and Economic Science.

Aid in obtaining and identifying photographs was provided by Dr. Daniel T. Williams, university archivist of Tuskegee University; Le Dzung, press attaché of the Permanent Mission of the Socialist Republic of Vietnam to the United Nations; G.M. Cookson; and the Friends of the Pathfinder Mural.

Steve Clark
December 1990

About the cover

The cover portrait of Malcolm X was painted by artist and sculptor Carole Byard. It forms part of the Pathfinder Mural, a six-story mural on the building that houses the Pathfinder offices in Lower Manhattan. Byard also painted portraits of antislavery fighters Harriet Tubman and Sojourner Truth on the mural.

The Pathfinder Mural, dedicated on November 19, 1989, was painted by an international volunteer team of eighty artists from twenty countries. Along with Malcolm X, it features portraits of other revolutionary and working-class leaders whose speeches and writings are published by Pathfinder.

About the artist

Carole Byard teaches at Parsons School of Design in New York City. Her art was influenced by travels in Africa in 1972 and 1977. She has exhibited in several anti-apartheid shows as well as shows on Black history and culture, winning numerous awards for her painting, sculpture, and illustrations. The illustrator of a dozen children's books, she is currently working on "Presence and Perception," a series of sculptures. Byard is active in Coast to Coast: National Women Artists of Color.

I'm not an American, I'm a victim of Americanism

I'm not an American, I'm a victim of Americanism

UNIVERSITY OF GHANA, MAY 13, 1964

The remarks that follow were made at the University of Ghana in Legon at a meeting sponsored by the Marxist Forum. The original title of the talk was "The Plight of 22 Million Afro-Americans in the United States." The audience, which filled the university's Great Hall, was the largest that Malcolm X addressed in Africa.

The talk was part of a week-long tour in Ghana that was organized by the Malcolm X Committee, made up of Afro-Americans living in that country. During his visit, Malcolm X met with Ghanaian president Kwame Nkrumah and spoke with ambassadors of at least fifteen countries of Africa, Asia, and Latin America. He also addressed members of parliament and the Kwame Nkrumah Ideological Institute, gave a press conference, and was honored at dinners given by the Cuban and Chinese ambassadors.

As a result of Malcolm X's trip to Ghana, a chapter of the Organization of Afro-American Unity was set up, composed of U.S. Blacks living there.[1]

I intend for my talk to be very informal, because our position in America is an informal position, [*Laughter*] and I find that it is very difficult to use formal terms to describe a very informal position. No condition of any people on earth is more deplorable than the condition, or plight, of the twenty-two million Black people in America. And our condition is so deplorable because we are in a country that professes to be a democracy and professes to be striving to give justice and freedom and equality to everyone who is born under its constitution. If we were born in South Africa or in Angola or some part of this earth where they don't profess to be for freedom,[2] that would be another thing; but when we are born in a country that stands up and represents itself as the leader of the Free World, and you still have to beg and crawl just to get a chance to drink a cup of coffee, then the condition is very deplorable indeed.

So tonight, so that you will understand me and why I speak as I do, it should probably be pointed out at the outset that I am not a politician. I don't know anything about politics. I'm from America but I'm not an American. I didn't go there of my own free choice. [*Applause*] If I were an American there would be no problem, there'd be no need for legislation or civil rights or anything else. So I just try to face the fact as it actually is and come to this meeting as one of the victims of America, one of the victims of Americanism, one of the victims of democracy, one of the victims of a very hypocritical system that is going all over this earth today representing itself as being qualified to tell other people how to run their country when they can't get the dirty things that are going on in their own country straightened out. [*Applause*]

So if someone else from America comes to you to speak, they're probably speaking as Americans, and they speak as people who see America through the eyes of an American. And usually those types of persons refer to America, or that which exists in America, as the American Dream. But for the twenty million of us in America who are of African descent, it is not an American dream; it's an American nightmare. [*Laughter*]

I don't feel that I am a visitor in Ghana or in any part of Africa. I feel that I am at home. I've been away for four hundred years, [*Laughter*] but not of my own volition, not of my own will. Our people didn't go to America on the *Queen Mary*, we didn't go by Pan American, and we didn't go to America on the *Mayflower*. We went in slave ships, we went in chains. We weren't immigrants to America, we were cargo for purposes of a system that was bent upon making a profit. So this is the category or level of which I speak. I may not speak it in the language many of you would use, but I think you will understand the meaning of my terms.

When I was in Ibadan [in Nigeria] at the University of Ibadan last Friday night, the students there gave me a new name, which I go for—meaning I like it. [*Laughter*] "Omowale," which they say means in Yoruba—if I am pronouncing that correctly, and if I am not pronouncing it correctly it's because I haven't had a chance to pronounce it for four hundred years [*Laughter*]—which means in that dialect, "The child has returned." It was an honor for me to be referred to as a child who had sense enough to return to the land of his forefathers—to his fatherland and to his motherland. Not sent back here by the State Department, [*Laughter*] but come back here of my own free will. [*Applause*]

I am happy and I imagine, since it is the policy that whenever a Black man leaves America and travels in any part of Africa, or Asia, or Latin America and says things contrary to what the American propaganda machine turns out, usually he finds upon his return home that his passport is lifted.[3] Well, if they had not wanted me to say the things I am saying, they should never have given me a passport in the first place. The policy usually is the lifting of the passport. Now I am not here to condemn America, I am not here to make America look bad, but I am here to tell you the truth about the situation that Black people in America find themselves confronted with. And if truth condemns America, then she stands condemned. [*Applause*]

This is the most beautiful continent that I've ever seen; it's the richest continent I've ever seen, and strange as it may seem, I find many white Americans here smiling in the faces of our African brothers like they have been loving them all of the time. [*Laughter and applause*] The fact is, these same whites who in America spit in our faces, the same whites who in America club us brutally, the same whites who in America sic their dogs upon us, just because we want to be free human beings, the same whites who turn their water hoses upon our women and our babies because we want to integrate with them, are over here in Africa smiling in your face trying to integrate with *you*. [*Laughter*]

I had to write a letter back home yesterday and tell some of my friends that if American Negroes want integration, they should come to Africa, because more white people over here—white Americans, that is—look like they are for integration than there is in the entire American country. [*Laughter*] But actually what it is, they want to integrate with the wealth that they know is here—the untapped natural resources which exceed the wealth of any continent on this earth today.

When I was coming from Lagos to Accra Sunday, I was riding on an airplane with a white man who represented some of the interests, you know, that are interested in Africa. And he admitted—at least it was his impression—that our people in Africa didn't know how to measure wealth, that they worship wealth in terms of gold and silver, not in terms of the natural resources that are in the earth, and that as long as the Americans or other imperialists or twentieth-century colonialists could continue to make the Africans measure wealth in terms of gold and silver, they never would have an opportunity to really measure the value of the wealth that is in the soil, and would continue to think that it is *they* who need the Western powers instead of thinking that it is the Western powers who need the people and the continent that is known as Africa. The thing is, I hope I don't mess up anybody's politics or anybody's plots or plans or schemes, but then I think that it can be well proved and backed up.

Ghana is one of the most progressive nations on the African continent primarily because it has one of the most progressive leaders and most progressive presidents. [*Applause*] The president of this nation has done something that no American, no white American, wants to see done—well, I should say "no American" because all the Americans over there are white Americans.

President Nkrumah is doing something there that the government in America does not like to see done, and that is he's restoring the African image. He is making the African proud of the African image; and whenever the African becomes proud of the African image and this positive image is projected abroad, then the Black man in America, who up to now has had nothing but a negative image of Africa—automatically the image that the Black man in America has of his African brothers changes from negative to positive, and the image that the Black man in America has of himself will also change from negative to positive.

And the American racists know that they can rule the African in America, the African-American in America, only as long as we have a negative image of ourselves. So they keep us with a negative image of Africa. And they also know that the day that the image of Africa is changed from negative to positive, automatically the attitude of twenty-two million Africans in America will also change from negative to positive.

And one of the most important efforts to change the image of the African is being made right here in Ghana. And the Ghanaian personality can be picked right out of any group of Africans anywhere on this planet, because you see nothing in him that reflects any kind of feeling of inferiority or anything of that sort. And as long as you have a president who teaches you that you can do anything that anybody else under the sun can do, you got a good man. [*Applause*]

Not only that, we who live in America have learned to measure Black men: the object we use to measure him is the attitude of America toward him. When we find a Black man who's always receiving the praise of the Americans, we become suspicious of him. When we find a Black man who receives honors and all kinds of plaques and beautiful phrases and words from America, we immediately begin to suspect that person. Because it has been our experience that the Americans don't praise any Black man who is really working for the benefit of the Black man, because they realize that when you begin to work in earnest to do things that are good for the people on the African continent, all the good you do for people on the African continent has got to be against someone else, because someone else up to now has benefited from the labor and the wealth of the people on this continent. So our yardstick in measuring these various leaders is to find out what the Americans think about them. And these leaders over here who are receiving the praise and pats on the back from the Americans, you can just flush the toilet and let them go right down the drain. [*Laughter*]

This president here is disliked. Don't think that it's just the American press, it's the government. In America when you find a concerted effort of the press to always speak in a bad way about an African leader, usually that press is actually reflecting government opinion. But America is a very shrewd government. If it knows that its own governmental position will cause a negative reaction from the people that it wants to continue to exploit, it will pretend to have a free press and at the same time sic that free press on a real African leader and stand on the sideline and say that this is not government policy. But everything that happens in America is government policy. [*Laughter*]

Not only is the president of this country disliked, the president of Algeria, Ben Bella, is disliked because he is revolutionary, he's for freedom of everybody. [Egyptian president] Nasser is disliked because he's for freedom of everybody. All of them are referred to as dictators. As soon as they get the mass of their people behind them, they're a dictator. As soon as they have unity of their people in their country, they're a dictator. If there is no division, fighting, and squabbling going on, the leader of that country is a dictator if he is an African; but as long as it is in America, he's just an American president who has the support of the people. [*Laughter and applause*]

I am coming to America in a minute, but I just want to comment on our relations I've noticed since being here. I heard that there is a conflict among some of our brothers and sisters over here concerning whether or not it's advisable for the government to play such a prominent role in guiding the education—the curriculum and what not—of the people of the country and in the various universities. Yes, anytime you have a people who have been colonized for as long as our people have been colonized, and you tell them now they can vote, they will spend all night arguing and never get anywhere. Everything needs to be controlled until the colonial mentality has been completely destroyed, and when that colonial mentality has been destroyed at least to the point where they know what they are voting for, then you give them a chance to vote on this and vote on that. But we have this trouble in America, as well as other areas where colonialism has existed, the only way they can practice or apply democratic practices is through advice and counsel.

So my own honest, humble opinion is, anytime you want to come out from under a colonial mentality, let the government set up the educational system and educate you in the direction or way they want you to go in; and then after your understanding is up to the level where it should be, you can stand around and argue or philosophize or something of that sort. [*Laughter and applause*]

There is probably no more enlightened leader on the African continent than President Nkrumah, because he lived in America. He knows what it is like there. He could not live in that land as long as he did and be disillusioned, or confused, or be deceived. Anytime you think that America is the land of the free, you come there and take off your national dress and be mistaken for an American Negro, and you will find out you're not in the land of the free. [*Applause*] America is a colonial power. She is just as much a colonial power in 1964 as France, Britain, Portugal, and all these other European countries were in 1864. She's a twentieth-century colonial power; she's a modern colonial power, and she has colonized twenty-two million African-Americans. While there are only eleven million Africans colonized in South Africa, four or five million colonized in Angola, there are twenty-two million Africans colonized in America right now on May 13, 1964. What is second-class citizenship if nothing but twentieth-century colonialism? They don't want you to know that slavery still exists, so rather than call it slavery they call it second-class citizenship.

Either you are a citizen or you are not a citizen at all. If you are a citizen, you are free; if you are not a citizen, you are a slave. And the American government is afraid to admit that she never gave freedom to the Black man in America and won't even admit that the Black man in America is not free, is not a citizen, and doesn't have his rights. She skillfully camouflages it under these pretty terms of second-class citizenship. It's colonialism, neocolonialism, imperialism . . . [*Inaudible*] [*Laughter*]

One of our brothers just landed here today from New York. He told me that when he left New York, the police were walking in Harlem six abreast. Why? Because Harlem is about to explode. You know what I mean by "Harlem"? Harlem is the most famous city on this earth; there is no city on the African continent with as many Africans as Harlem. In Harlem they call it little Africa, and when you walk through Harlem, you're in Ibadan, everyone there looks just like you. And today the police were out in force, with their clubs. They don't have police dogs in Harlem, 'cause those kind of people who live in Harlem don't allow police dogs to come in Harlem. [*Laughter*] That's the point, they don't allow police dogs to come in Harlem. . . . [*Inaudible*]

They are troubled with the existence of little gangs who have been going around killing people, killing white people.[4] Well now, they project it abroad as an antiwhite gang. No, it's not an antiwhite gang, it's an *antioppression* gang. It's an *antifrustration* gang. They don't know what else to do. They've been waiting for the government to solve their problems; they've been waiting for the president to solve their problems; they've been waiting for the Senate and the Congress and the Supreme Court to solve their problems; they've been waiting for Negro leaders to solve their problems; and all they hear are a lot of pretty words. So they become frustrated and don't know what to do. So they do the only thing they know how: they do the same thing the Americans did when they got frustrated with the British in 1776—liberty or death.

This is what the Americans did; they didn't turn the other cheek to the British. No, they had an old man named Patrick Henry who said, "Liberty or death!" I never heard them refer to him as an advocate of violence; they say he's one of the Founding Fathers, because he had sense to say, "Liberty or death!"

And there is a growing tendency among Black Americans today, who are able to see that they don't have freedom—they are reaching the point now where they are ready to tell the Man no matter what the odds are against them, no matter what the cost is, it's liberty or death. If this is the land of the free, then give us some freedom. If this is the land of justice, then give us some justice. And if this is the land of equality, give us some equality. This is the growing temper of the Black American, of the African-American, of which there are twenty-two million.

Am I justified in talking like this? Let me see. I was in Cleveland, Ohio, just two months ago when this white clergyman was killed by the bulldozer.[5] I was in Cleveland, I was there. Now you know if a white man in the garb, in the outfit, the costume, or whatever you want to call it, of a priest . . . [*Inaudible*] if they run over him with a bulldozer, what will they do to a Black man? They run over someone who *looks* like them who is demonstrating for freedom, what chance does a Black man have? This wasn't in Mississippi, this was in Cleveland in the North. This is the type of experience the Black man in America is faced with every day. . . . [*Inaudible*]

*Any means necessary
to bring about
freedom*

*The oppressed
masses of the world
cry out for action
against the
common oppressor*

Any means necessary
to bring about freedom

OXFORD UNIVERSITY, DECEMBER 3, 1964

The following remarks were given as part of a debate sponsored by the Oxford Union, a student organization at Britain's Oxford University. The debate was televised to an audience of millions by Britain's national network, the British Broadcasting Corporation.

The proposition under debate was "Extremism in defense of liberty is no vice, moderation in the pursuit of justice is no virtue," a statement popularized in July 1964 by Barry Goldwater in his speech accepting the Republican Party nomination for president of the United States.

The fifth of six speakers in the debate, Malcolm X took the floor immediately following Conservative Party member of Parliament Humphry Berkeley, who opposed the motion. The other two opposing speakers were Lord Stoneham, a Labour Party member of the House of Lords, and Cambridge student union president Christie Davies. Speaking for the proposition besides Malcolm X were Eric Abrahams, a student from Jamaica and president of the Oxford Union; and Scottish poet and Communist Party member Hugh MacDiarmid. Tariq Ali, a student of Pakistani origin, chaired. There was no question period.

The first part of Malcolm X's remarks is not available. According to press accounts, he began by denouncing the bombing of defenseless villages in the Congo (today Zaire) that year, a question he also takes up in other speeches in the present collection.

The audience, which included many students originally from Africa and Asia, greeted Malcolm's remarks with long and enthusiastic applause. The minutes of the meeting record that in a vote held after the debate, the motion Malcolm X was defending received 137 votes to 228 against.

Y ou make my point, [*Laughter*] that as long as a white man does it, it's all right. A Black man is supposed to have no feelings. [*Applause*] So when a Black man strikes back, he's an extremist. He's supposed to sit passively and have no feelings, be nonviolent, and love his enemy. No matter what kind of attack, be it verbal or otherwise, he's supposed to take it. But if he stands up and in any way tries to defend himself, [*Malcolm laughs*] then he's an extremist. [*Laughter and applause*]

No. I think that the speaker who preceded me is getting exactly what he asked for. [*Laughter*] My reason for believing in extremism—intelligently directed extremism, extremism in defense of liberty, extremism in quest of justice—is because I firmly believe in my heart that the day that the Black man takes an uncompromising step and realizes that he's within his rights, when his own freedom is being jeopardized, to use any means necessary to bring about his freedom or put a halt to that injustice, I don't think he'll be by himself.

I live in America, where there are only 22 million Blacks against probably 160 million whites. One of the reasons that I'm in no way reluctant or hesitant to do whatever is necessary to see that Black people do something to protect themselves [is that] I honestly believe that the day that they do, many whites will have more respect for them. And there will be more whites on their side than are now on their side with this little wishy-washy "love-thy-enemy" approach that they've been using up to now.

And if I'm wrong, then you are racialists. [*Malcolm laughs; laughter and applause from the audience*]

As I said earlier, in my conclusion, I'm a Muslim. I believe in the religion of Islam. I believe in Allah, I believe in Muhammad, I believe in all of the prophets. I believe in fasting, prayer, charity, and that which is incumbent upon a Muslim to fulfill in order to be a Muslim. In April I was fortunate to make the hajj to Mecca, and went back again in September to try and carry out my religious functions and requirements.

But at the same time that I believe in that religion, I have to point out I'm also an American Negro, and I live in a society whose social system is based upon the castration of the Black man, whose political system is based on castration of the Black man, and whose economy is based upon the castration of the Black man. A society which, in 1964, has more subtle, deceptive, deceitful methods to make the rest of the world think that it's cleaning up its house, while at the same time the same things are happening to us in 1964 that happened in 1954, 1924, and in 1984.

They came up with what they call a civil rights bill in 1964, supposedly to solve our problem, and after the bill was signed, three civil rights workers were murdered in cold blood.[6] And the FBI head, [J. Edgar] Hoover, admits that they know who did it. They've known ever since it happened, and they've done nothing about it. Civil rights bill down the drain. No matter how many bills pass, Black people in that country where I'm from—still, our lives are not worth two cents. And the government has shown its inability, or its unwillingness, to do whatever is necessary to protect life and property where the Black American is concerned.

So my contention is that whenever a people come to the conclusion that the government which they have supported proves itself unwilling or proves itself unable to protect our lives and protect our property because we have the wrong color skin, we are not human beings unless we ourselves band together and do whatever, however, whenever is necessary to see that our lives and our property is protected. And I doubt that any person in here would refuse to do the same thing, were he in the same position. Or I should say, were he in the same condition. [*Applause*]

Just one step farther to see, am I justified in this stand? And I say, I'm speaking as a Black man from America, which is a racist society. No matter how much you hear it talk about democracy, it's as racist as South Africa or as racist as Portugal, or as racist as any other racialist society on this earth. The only difference between it and South Africa: South Africa preaches separation and practices separation; America preaches integration and practices segregation. This is the only difference. They don't practice what they preach, whereas South Africa preaches and practices the same thing. I have more respect for a man who lets me know where he stands, even if he's wrong, than one who comes up like an angel and is nothing but a devil. [*Applause*]

The system of government that America has consists of committees. There are sixteen senatorial committees that govern the country and twenty congressional committees. Ten of the sixteen senatorial committees are in the hands of southern racialists, senators who are racialists. Thirteen of the twenty—well this was before the last election, I think it's even more so now. Ten of the sixteen committees, senatorial committees, are in the hands of senators who are southern racialists. Thirteen of the twenty congressional committees were in the hands of southern congressmen who are racialists. Which means out of the thirty-six committees that govern the foreign and domestic direction of that government, twenty-three are in the hands of southern racialists—men who in no way believe in the equality of man, and men who would do anything within their power to see that the Black man never gets to the same seat or to the same level that they are on.

The reason that these men from that area have that type of power is because America has a seniority system. And these who have that seniority have been there longer than anyone else because the Black people in the areas where they live can't vote. And it is only because the Black man is deprived of his vote that puts these men in positions of power, that gives them such influence in the government beyond their actual intellectual or political ability, or even beyond the number of people from the areas that they represent.

So we can see in that country that no matter what the federal government professes to be doing, the power of the federal government lies in these committees. And any time any kind of legislation is proposed to benefit the Black man or give the Black man his just due, we find it is locked up in these committees right here. And when they let something through the committee, usually it is so chopped up and fixed up that by the time it becomes law, it's a law that can't be enforced.

Another example is the Supreme Court desegregation decision that was handed down in 1954.[7] This is a law, and they have not been able to implement this law in New York City, or in Boston, or in Cleveland, or Chicago, or the northern cities. And my contention is that any time you have a country, supposedly a democracy, supposedly the land of the free and the home of the brave, and it can't enforce laws—even in the northernmost, cosmopolitan, and progressive part of it—that will benefit a Black man, if those laws can't be enforced or that law can't be enforced, how much heart do you think we will get when they pass some civil rights legislation which only involves more laws? If they can't enforce this law, they will never enforce those laws.

So my contention is that we are faced with a racialistic society, a society in which they are deceitful, deceptive, and the only way we can bring about a change is to talk the kind of language—speak the language that they understand. The racialists never understand a peaceful language. The racialist never understands the nonviolent language. The racialist we have, he's spoken his language to us for four hundred years.

We have been the victim of his brutality. We are the ones who face his dogs that tear the flesh from our limbs, only because we want to enforce the Supreme Court decision. We are the ones who have our skulls crushed, not by the Ku Klux Klan but by policemen, only because we want to enforce what they call the Supreme Court decision. We are the ones upon whom water hoses are turned, with pressure so hard that it rips the clothes from our backs—not men, but the clothes from the backs of women and children. You've seen it yourselves. Only because we want to enforce what they call the law.

Well, any time you live in a society supposedly based upon law, and it doesn't enforce its own law because the color of a man's skin happens to be wrong, then I say those people are justified to resort to any means necessary to bring about justice where the government can't give them justice. [*Prolonged applause*]

I don't believe in any form of unjustified extremism. But I believe that when a man is exercising extremism, a human being is exercising extremism in defense of liberty for human beings, it's no vice. And when one is moderate in the pursuit of justice for human beings, I say he's a sinner.

And I might add, in my conclusion— In fact, America is one of the best examples, when you read its history, about extremism. Old Patrick Henry said, "Liberty or death!" That's extreme, very extreme. [*Laughter and applause*]

I read once, passingly, about a man named Shakespeare. I only read about him passingly, but I remember one thing he wrote that kind of moved me. He put it in the mouth of Hamlet, I think it was, who said, "To be or not to be"—he was in doubt about something. [*Laughter*] "Whether it was nobler in the mind of man to suffer the slings and arrows of outrageous fortune"—moderation— "or to take up arms against a sea of troubles and by opposing end them."

And I go for that. If you take up arms, you'll end it. But if you sit around and wait for the one who's in power to make up his mind that he should end it, you'll be waiting a long time.

And in my opinion the young generation of whites, Blacks, browns, whatever else there is—you're living at a time of extremism, a time of revolution, a time when there's got to be a change. People in power have misused it, and now there has to be a change and a better world has to be built, and the only way it's going to be built is with extreme methods. And I for one will join in with anyone, I don't care what color you are, as long as you want to change this miserable condition that exists on this earth.

Thank you. [*Applause*]

"I think young people here can find a powerful example in the young simbas in the Congo and the young fighters in South Vietnam."

Above: Vietnamese youth demonstrate. Banner reads, "Chi Lang village youth volunteer in anti-U.S. war of national salvation." Sign at left says, "Nothing is more precious than independence and freedom."

The oppressed masses of the world cry out for action against the common oppressor

LONDON SCHOOL OF ECONOMICS, FEBRUARY 11, 1965

The speech that follows was given at the London School of Economics to a meeting called by the school's Africa Society. An initial section of Malcolm X's remarks is unavailable.

A central theme of Malcolm X's talk was the U.S. intervention against liberation forces in the Congo (today Zaire). The Congo had declared its independence from Belgium June 30, 1960. It was one of almost thirty former colonies in Africa that won political independence between 1956 and 1964. White-minority rule continued, however, across most of southern Africa: in the Portuguese colonies of Angola and Mozambique, in Southern Rhodesia (today Zimbabwe), in South-West Africa (today Namibia), and in South Africa.

The first independent government of the Congo was headed by Patrice Lumumba, who had led the liberation struggle there. Washington and its allies moved swiftly to destabilize this government, sending Belgian and United Nations troops into the capital, Léopoldville (today Kinshasa). They also backed a proimperialist breakaway regime set up by Moise Tshombe in a southern province.

The U.S.-led intervention succeeded by late 1960 in winning over a faction within the Congolese government, and Lumumba was deposed. He was later arrested and handed over to Tshombe's forces, who murdered him in January 1961.

In 1964 Tshombe was installed in Léopoldville as prime minister of the central government. Lumumba's followers, centered in the eastern town of Stanleyville (today Kisangani) and the surrounding Oriental and Kivu provinces, led a revolt against Tshombe's imperialist-backed government. Belgian troops and hired mercenaries were sent in to crush the uprising. Washington later admitted that U.S. planes flown by U.S. pilots "under contract" to the Tshombe regime had taken part in the operation.

That element is the one that controls or has strong influence in the power structure. It uses the press skillfully to feed statistics to the public to make it appear that the rate of crime in the Black community, or community of nonwhite people, is at such a high level. It gives the impression or the image that everyone in that community is criminal.

And as soon as the public accepts the fact that the dark-skinned community consists largely of criminals or people who are dirty, then it makes it possible for the power structure to set up a police-state system. Which will make it permissible in the minds of even the well-meaning white public for them to come in and use all kinds of police methods to brutally suppress the struggle on the part of these people against segregation, discrimination, and other acts that are unleashed against them that are absolutely unjust.

They use the press to set up this police state, and they use the press to make the white public accept whatever they do to the dark-skinned public. They do that here in London right now with the constant reference to the West Indian population and the Asian population having a high rate of crime or having a tendency toward dirtiness. They have all kinds of negative characteristics that they project to make the white public draw back, or to make the white public be apathetic when police-state-like methods are used in these areas to suppress the people's honest and just struggle against discrimination and other forms of segregation.

A good example of how they do it in New York: Last summer, when the Blacks were rioting—the riots, actually they weren't riots in the first place; they were reactions against police brutality.[8] And when the Afro-Americans reacted against the brutal measures that were executed against them by the police, the press all over the world projected them as rioters. When the store windows were broken in the Black community, immediately it was made to appear that this was being done not by people who were reacting over civil rights violations, but they gave the impression that these were hoodlums, vagrants, criminals, who wanted nothing other than to get into the stores and take the merchandise.

But this is wrong. In America the Black community in which we live is not owned by us. The landlord is white. The merchant is white. In fact, the entire economy of the Black community in the States is controlled by someone who doesn't even live there. The property that we live in is owned by someone else. The store that we trade with is operated by someone else. And these are the people who suck the economic blood of our community.

And being in a position to suck the economic blood of our community, they control the radio programs that cater to us, they control the newspapers, the advertising, that cater to us. They control our minds. They end up controlling our civic organizations. They end up controlling us economically, politically, socially, mentally, and every other kind of way. They suck our blood like vultures.

And when you see the Blacks react, since the people who do this aren't there, they react against their property. The property is the only thing that's there. And they destroy it. And you get the impression over here that because they are destroying the property where they live, that they are destroying their own property. No. They can't get to the Man, so they get at what he owns. [*Laughter*]

This doesn't say it's intelligent. But whoever heard of a sociological explosion that was done intelligently and politely? And this is what you're trying to make the Black man do. You're trying to drive him into a ghetto and make him the victim of every kind of unjust condition imaginable. Then when he explodes, you want him to explode politely! [*Laughter*] You want him to explode according to somebody's ground rules. Why, you're dealing with the wrong man, and you're dealing with him at the wrong time in the wrong way.

Another example of how this imagery is mastered, at the international level, is the recent situation in the

Congo. Here we have an example of planes dropping bombs on defenseless African villages. When a bomb is dropped on an African village, there's no way of defending the people from the bomb. The bomb doesn't make a distinction between men and women. That bomb is dropped on men, women, children, and babies. Now it has not been in any way a disguised fact that planes have been dropping bombs on Congolese villages all during the entire summer. There is no outcry. There is no concern. There is no sympathy. There is no urge on the part of even the so-called progressive element to try and bring a halt to this mass murder. Why?

Because all the press had to do was use that shrewd propaganda word that these villages were in "rebel-held" territory. "Rebel-held," what does that mean? That's an enemy, so anything that they do to those people is all right. You cease to think of the women and the children and the babies in the so-called rebel-held territory as human beings. So that anything that is done to them is done with justification. And the progressives, the liberals don't even make any outcry. They sit twiddling their thumbs, as if they were captivated by this press imagery that has been mastered here in the West also.

They refer to the pilots that are dropping the bombs on these babies as "American-trained, anti-Castro Cuban pilots." As long as they are American-trained, this is supposed to put the stamp of approval on it, because America is your ally. As long as they are anti-Castro Cubans, since Castro is supposed to be a monster and these pilots are against Castro, anybody else they are against is also all right. So the American planes with American bombs being piloted by American-trained pilots, dropping American bombs on Black people, Black babies, Black children, destroying them completely—which is nothing but mass murder—goes absolutely unnoticed. . . . [*Gap in tape*]

They take this man Tshombe—I guess he's a man—and try and make him acceptable to the public by using the press to refer to him as the only one who can unite the

Congo. Imagine, a murderer—not an ordinary murderer, a murderer of a prime minister, the murderer of the rightful prime minister of the Congo—and yet they want to force him upon the people of the Congo, through Western manipulation and Western pressures. The United States, the country that I come from, pays his salary. They openly admit that they pay his salary. And in saying this, I don't want you to think that I come here to make an anti-American speech. [*Laughter*] I wouldn't come here for that. I come here to make a speech, to tell you the truth. And if the truth is anti-American, then blame the truth, don't blame me. [*Laughter*]

He's propped up by American dollars. The salaries of the hired killers from South Africa that he uses to kill innocent Congolese are paid by American dollars. Which means that I come from a country that is busily sending the Peace Corps to Nigeria while sending hired killers to the Congo. [*Laughter*] The government is not consistent; something is not right there. And it starts some of my African brothers and sisters that have been so happy to see the Peace Corps landing on their shores to take another look at that thing, and see what it really is. [*From the audience: "What is it?"*] Exactly what it says: Peace Corps, get a piece of their country. [*Laughter and applause*]

So what the press does with its skillful ability to create this imagery, it uses its pages to whip up this hysteria in the white public. And as soon as the hysteria of the white public reaches the proper degree, they will begin to work on the sympathy of the white public. And once the sympathy reaches the proper degree, then they put forth their program, knowing that they are going to get the support of the gullible white public in whatever they do. And what they are going to do is criminal. And what they are doing is criminal.

How do they do it? If you recall reading in the paper, they never talked about the Congolese who were being slaughtered. But as soon as a few whites, the lives of a

"There is no better example of criminal activity against an oppressed people than the role the U.S. has been playing in the Congo."

Above: Mercenary views the body of a rebel fighter in the Congo, 1964.
• PHOTO: UPI

Left: Patrice Lumumba, prime minister of the Congo. He was ousted from power and assassinated with Washington's complicity.
• PHOTO: UNITED NATIONS

few whites were at stake, they began to speak of "white hostages," "white missionaries," "white priests," "white nuns"—as if a white life, one white life, was of such greater value than a Black life, than a thousand Black lives. They showed you their open contempt for the lives of the Blacks, and their deep concern for the lives of the whites. This is the press. And after the press had gotten the whites all whipped up, then anything that the Western powers wanted to do against these defenseless, innocent freedom fighters from the eastern provinces of the Congo, the white public went along with it. [*From the audience: "It's true."*] They know it's true.

So to get towards the end of that, what it has done, just in press manipulation, the Western governments have permitted themselves to get trapped, in a sense, in backing Tshombe, the same as the United States is trapped over there in South Vietnam.[9] If she goes forward she loses, if she backs up she loses. She's getting bogged down in the Congo in the same way.

Because no African troops win victories for Tshombe. They never have. The only war, the only battles won by the African troops, in the African revolution, in the Congo area, were those won by the freedom fighters from the Oriental province. They won battles with spears, stones, twigs. They won battles because their heart was in what they were doing. But Tshombe's men from the central Congo government never won any battles. And it was for this reason that he had to import these white mercenaries, the paid killers, to win some battles for him. Which means that Tshombe's government can only stay in power with white help, with white troops.

Well, there will come a time when he won't be able to recruit any more mercenaries, and the Western powers, who are really behind him, will then have to commit their own troops openly. Which means you will then be bogged down in the Congo the same as you're bogged down over there now in South Vietnam. And you can't win in the Congo. If you can't win in South Vietnam, you know you can't win in the Congo.

Just let me see. You think you can win in South Vietnam? The French were deeply entrenched. The French were deeply entrenched in Vietnam for a hundred years or so. They had the best weapons of warfare, a highly mechanized army, everything that you would need. And the guerrillas come out of the rice paddies with nothing but sneakers on and a rifle [*Laughter*] and a bowl of rice, nothing but gym shoes—tennis shoes—and a rifle and a bowl of rice. And you know what they did in Dien Bien Phu. They ran the French out of there.[10] And if the French were deeply entrenched and couldn't stay there, then how do you think someone else is going to stay there, who is not even there yet. [*From the audience: "You'll have it happen again."*] We'll get to you in a minute. [*Laughter*] I'm going to sit down and you can tell all you want to say. You can even come up here. [*From the audience: "Yes, I was just making the point that it was Chinese—"*] Make it later on. [*Laughter*]

Yes, all of them are brothers. They were still—they had a bowl of rice and a rifle and some shoes. I don't care whether they came from China or South Vietnam. [*The person from the audience continues interrupting; someone else responds, "Shut up!"*] And the French aren't there anymore. We don't care how they did it; they're not there anymore. [*Malcolm laughs; laughter from the audience*] The same thing will happen in the Congo.

See, the African revolution must proceed onward, and one of the reasons that the Western powers are fighting so hard and are trying to cloud the issue in the Congo is that it's not a humanitarian project. It's not a feeling or sense of humanity that makes them want to go in and save some hostages, but there are bigger stakes.

They realize not only that the Congo is a source of mineral wealth, minerals that they need. But the Congo is so situated strategically, geographically, that if it falls into the hands of a genuine African government that has the hopes and aspirations of the African people at heart, then it will be possible for the Africans to put their own soldiers right on the border of Angola and wipe the Portuguese out of there overnight.

So that if the Congo falls, Mozambique and Angola must fall. And when they fall, suddenly you have to deal with Ian Smith.[11] He won't be there overnight once you can put some troops on his borders. [*Applause*] Oh yes. Which means it will only be a matter of time before they will be right on the border with South Africa, and then they can talk the type of language that the South Africans understand. And this is the only language that they understand. [*Applause*]

I might point out right here and now—and I say it bluntly—that you have had a generation of Africans who actually have believed that they could negotiate, negotiate, negotiate, and eventually get some kind of independence. But you're getting a new generation that is being born right now, and they are beginning to think with their own mind and see that you can't negotiate upon freedom nowadays. If something is yours by right, then you fight for it or shut up. If you can't fight for it, then forget it. [*Applause*]

So we in the West have a stake in the African revolution. We have a stake for this reason: as long as the African continent was dominated by enemies, and as long as it was dominated by colonial powers, those colonial powers were enemies of the African people. They were enemies to the African continent. They meant the African people no good, they did the African people no good, they did the African continent no good.

And then in the position that they were, they were the ones who created the image of the African continent and the African people. They created that continent and those people in a negative image. And they projected this negative image abroad. They projected an image of Africa in the people abroad that was very hateful, extremely hateful.

And because it was hateful, there are over a hundred

million of us of African heritage in the West [who] looked at that hateful image and didn't want to be identified with it. We shunned it, and not because it was something to be shunned. But we believed the image that had been created of our own homeland by the enemy of our own homeland. And in hating that image we ended up hating ourselves without even realizing it. [*Applause*]

Why? Because once we in the West were made to hate Africa and hate the African, why, the chain-reaction effect was it had to make us end up hating ourselves. You can't hate the roots of the tree without hating the tree, without ending up hating the tree. You can't hate your origin without ending up hating yourself. You can't hate the land, your motherland, the place that you came from, and we can't hate Africa without ending up hating ourselves.

The Black man in the Western Hemisphere—in North America, Central America, South America, and in the Caribbean—is the best example of how one can be made, skillfully, to hate himself that you can find anywhere on this earth.

The reason you're having a problem with the West Indies right now is because they hate their origin. Because they don't want to accept their origin, they have no origin, they have no identity. They are running around here in search of an identity, and instead of trying to be what they are, they want to be Englishmen. [*Applause*] Which is not their fault, actually. Because in America our people are trying to be Americans, and in the islands you got them trying to be Englishmen, and nothing sounds more obnoxious than to find somebody from Jamaica running around here trying to outdo the Englishman with his Englishness. [*Laughter and applause*]

And I say that this is a very serious problem, because all of it stems from what the Western powers do to the image of the African continent and the African people. By making our people in the Western Hemisphere hate Africa, we ended up hating ourselves. We hated our African characteristics. We hated our African identity. We hated our African features. So much so that you would find those of us in the West who would hate the shape of our nose. We would hate the shape of our lips. We would hate the color of our skin and the texture of our hair. This was a reaction, but we didn't realize that it was a reaction.

Imagine now, somebody got nerve enough, some whites have the audacity to refer to *me* as a hate teacher. If I'm teaching someone to hate, I teach them to hate the Ku Klux Klan. But here in America, they have taught us to hate ourselves. To hate our skin, hate our hair, hate our features, hate our blood, hate what we are. Why, Uncle Sam is a master hate teacher, so much so that he makes somebody think he's teaching love, when he's teaching hate. When you make a man hate himself, why you really got it and gone. [*Laughter and applause*]

By skillfully making us hate Africa and, in turn, making us hate ourselves, hate our color and our blood, our color became a chain. Our color became to us a chain. It became a prison. It became something that was a shame, something that we felt held us back, kept us trapped.

So because we felt that our color had trapped us, had imprisoned us, had brought us down, we ended up hating the Black skin, which we felt was holding us back. We ended up hating the Black blood, which we felt was holding us back. This is the problem that the Black man in the West has had.

The African hasn't realized that this was the problem. And it was only as long as the African himself was held in bondage by the colonial powers, was kept from projecting any positive image of himself on our continent, something that we could look at proudly and then identify with—it was only as long as the African himself was kept down that we were kept down.

But to the same degree, during these recent years, that the African people have become independent, and they have gotten in a position on that continent to project their own image, their image has shifted from negative to positive. And to the same degree that it has shifted from negative to positive, you'll find that the image of the Black man in the West of himself has also shifted from negative to positive. To the same degree that the African has become uncompromising and militant in knowing what he wants, you will find that the Black man in the West has followed the same line.

Why? Because the same beat, the same heart, the same pulse that moves the Black man on the African continent—despite the fact that four hundred years have separated us from that mother continent, and an ocean of water has separated us from that mother continent—still, the same pulse that beats in the Black man on the African continent today is beating in the heart of the Black man in North America, Central America, South America, and in the Caribbean. Many of them don't know it, but it's true. [*Applause*]

As long as we hated our African blood, our African skin, our Africanness, we ended up feeling inferior, we felt inadequate, and we felt helpless. And because we felt so inferior and so inadequate and so helpless, instead of trying to stand on our own feet and do something for ourselves, we turned to the white man, thinking he was the only one who could do it for us. Because we were taught, we have been taught, that he was the personification of beauty and the personification of success.

At the Bandung Conference in nineteen fifty—[*From the audience: "five"*] five, [*Laughter*] one of the first and best steps toward real independence for nonwhite people took place. The people of Africa and Asia and Latin America were able to get together. They sat down, they realized that they had differences. They agreed not to place any emphasis any longer upon these differences, but to submerge the areas of differences and place emphasis upon areas where they had something in common.[12]

This agreement that was reached at Bandung produced the spirit of Bandung. So that the people who were oppressed, who had no jet planes, no nuclear weapons, no armies, no navies—and despite the fact that they didn't have this, their unity alone was sufficient to enable them, over a period of years, to maneuver and make it possible for other nations in Asia to become independent, and many more nations in Africa to become independent.

And by 1959, many of you will recall how colonialism on the African continent had already begun to collapse. It began to collapse because the spirit of African nationalism had been fanned from a spark to a roaring flame. And it made it impossible for the colonial powers to stay there by force. Formerly, when the Africans were fearful, the colonial powers could come up with a battleship, or threaten to land an army, or something like that, and the oppressed people would submit and go ahead being colonized for a while longer.

But by 1959 all of the fear had left the African continent and the Asian continent. And because this fear was gone, especially in regards to the colonial powers of Europe, it made it impossible for them to continue to stay in there by the same methods that they had employed up to that time.

So it's just like when a person is playing football. If he has the ball and he gets trapped, he doesn't throw the ball away, he passes it to some of his teammates who are in the clear. And in 1959, when France and Britain and Belgium and some of the others saw that they were trapped by the African nationalism on that continent, instead of throwing the ball of colonialism away, they passed it to the only one of their team that was in the clear—and that was Uncle Sam. [*Laughter*] Uncle Sam grabbed the ball [*Laughter and applause*] and has been running with it ever since. [*Laughter and applause*]

The one who picked it up, really, was John F. Kennedy. He was the shrewdest backfield runner that America has produced in a long time—oh yes he was. He was very tricky; he was intelligent; he was an intellectual; he surrounded himself with intellectuals who had a lot of foresight and a lot of cunning. The first thing they did was to give a reanalysis of the problem. They realized they were confronted with a new problem.

The newness of the problem was created by the fact that the Africans had lost all fear. There was no fear in them anymore. Therefore the colonial powers couldn't stay there by force, and America, the new colonial power, neocolonial power, or neoimperialist power, also couldn't stay there by force. So they come up with a "friendly" approach, a new approach which was friendly. Benevolent colonialism or philanthropic imperialism. [*Laughter*] They called it humanitarianism, or dollarism. And whereas the Africans could fight against colonialism, they found it difficult to fight against dollarism, or to condemn dollarism. It was all a token friendship, and all of the so-called benefits that were offered to the African countries were nothing but tokens.

But from '54 to '64 was the era of an emerging Africa, an independent Africa. And the impact of those independent African nations upon the civil rights struggle in the United States was tremendous. Number one, one of the first things the African revolution produced was rapid growth in a movement called the Black Muslim movement. The militancy that existed on the African continent was one of the main motivating factors in the rapid growth of the group known as the Black Muslim movement, to which I belonged. And the Black Muslim movement was one of the main ingredients in the entire civil rights struggle, although the movement itself never . . . [*Gap in tape*]

Martin Luther King has held Negroes in check up to recently. But he's losing his grip, he's losing his influence, he's losing his control.

I know you don't want me to say that. But, see, this is why you're in trouble. You want somebody to come and tell you that your house is safe, while you're sitting on a powder keg. [*Laughter and applause*] This is the mentality, this is the level of Western mentality today. Rather than face up to the facts concerning the danger that you're in, you would rather have someone come along and jive you and tell you that everything is all right and pack you to sleep. [*Laughter*] Why, the best thing that anybody can tell you is when they let you know how fed up with disillusionment and frustration the man in your house has become.

So to bring my talk to a conclusion, I must point out that just as John F. Kennedy realized the necessity of a new approach on the African problem—and I must say that it was during his administration that the United States gained so much influence on the African continent. They removed the other colonial powers and stepped in themselves with their benevolent, philanthropic, friendly approach. And they got just as firm a grip on countries on that continent as some of the colonial powers formerly had on that continent. Not only on the African continent but in Asia too. They did it with dollars.

They used a new approach on us in the States, also. Friendly. Whereas formerly they just outright denied us certain rights, they began to use a new, tricky approach. And this approach was to make it appear that they were making moves to solve our problems. They would pass bills, they would come up with Supreme Court decisions. The Supreme Court came up with what they called a desegregation decision in 1954—it hasn't been implemented yet; they can't even implement it in New York City, where I live—outlawing the segregated school system, supposedly to eliminate segregated schooling in Mississippi and Alabama and other places in the South. And they haven't even been able to implement this Supreme Court decision concerning the educational system in New York City and in Boston and some of the so-called liberal cities of the North.

This was all tokenism. They made the world think that they had desegregated the University of Mississippi. This shows you how deceitful they are. They took one Negro, named [James] Meredith, and took all of the world press down to show that they were going to solve the problem [*Laughter*] by putting Meredith in the University of Mis-

sissippi. I think it cost them something like $15 million
and they had to use about seven thousand troops—one or
the other—to put one Black man in the University of
Mississippi.

And then *Look* magazine came out with a story after-
wards showing the exposé where the attorney general—
at that time Robert Kennedy—had made a deal with
Governor Barnett. They were going to play a game on the
Negro. Barnett was the racist governor from Mississippi.
Kennedy was one of these shining liberal progressives—
Robert, that is. And they had made a deal, according to
Look magazine—which all belongs to the same setup, so
they must know what they are talking about. [*Laughter
and applause*] *Look* magazine said that Robert Kennedy
had told Barnett, "Now, since you want the white votes in
the South, what you do is you stand in the doorway and
pretend like you're going to keep Meredith out. And when
I come, I'm going to come with the marshals, and force
Meredith in. So you'll keep all the white votes in the
South, and I'll get all the Negro votes in the North."[13]
[*Laughter and applause*]

This is what we face in that country. And Kennedy is
supposed to be a liberal. He's supposed to be a friend of
the Negro. He's supposed to be the brother of John F.
Kennedy—all of them in the same family. You know, he
being the attorney general, he couldn't go down with that
kind of deal unless he had the permission of his older
brother, who was his older brother at that time.

So they come up only with tokenism. And this tokenism
that they give us benefits only a few. A few handpicked
Negroes gain from this; a few handpicked Negroes get
good jobs; a few handpicked Negroes get good homes or go
to a decent school. And then they use these handpicked
Negroes, they put 'em on television, blow 'em up, and
make it look like you got a whole lot of 'em, when you
only got one or two. [*Laughter*]

And this one or two is going to open up his mouth and
talk about how the problem is being solved. And the

whole world thinks that America's race problem is being solved, when actually the masses of Black people in America are still living in the ghettos and the slums; they still are the victims of inferior housing; they are still the victims of a segregated school system, which gives them inferior education. They are still victims, after they get that inferior education, where they can only get the worst form of jobs.

And they do this very skillfully to keep us trapped. They know that as long as they keep us undereducated, or with an inferior education, it's impossible for us to compete with them for job openings. And as long as we can't compete with them and get a decent job, we're trapped. We are low-wage earners. We have to live in a run-down neighborhood, which means our children go to inferior schools. They get inferior education. And when they grow up, they fall right into the same cycle again.

This is the American way. This is the American democracy that she tries to sell to the whole world as being that which will solve the problems of other people too. It's the worst form of hypocrisy that has ever been practiced by any government or society anywhere on this earth, since the beginning of time. And if I'm wrong you can— [*Applause*]

It is the African revolution that produced the Black Muslim movement. It was the Black Muslim movement that pushed the civil rights movement. And it was the civil rights movement that pushed the liberals out into the open, where today they are exposed as people who have no more concern for the rights of dark-skinned humanity than they do for any other form of humanity.

To bring my talk to a conclusion, all of this created a hot climate, a hot climate. And from 1963, '64 it reached its peak. Nineteen sixty-three was started out in America by all of the politicians talking about this being the hundredth year since the Emancipation Proclamation.[14] They were going to celebrate all over America "a century of progress in race relations." This is the way January and

February and March of 1963 started out.

And then Martin Luther King went into Birmingham, Alabama, just trying to get a few Negroes to be able to sit down at a lunch counter and drink an integrated cup of coffee. That's all he wanted. [*Laughter and applause*] That's all he wanted. They ended up putting him in jail. They ended up putting thousands of Negroes in jail. And many of you saw on television, in Birmingham, how the police had these big vicious dogs biting Black people. They were crushing the skulls of Black people. They had water hoses turned on our women, stripping off the clothes from our own women, from our children.

And the world saw this. The world saw what the world had thought was going to be a year which would celebrate a hundred years of progress toward good race relations between white and Black in the United States—they saw one of the most inhuman, savage displays there in that country.

Right after that, this was followed by the assassination of John F. Kennedy, all by the same problem, and Medgar Evers, another one by the same problem. And it ended in the bombing of a church in Alabama where four little girls, Christians, sitting in Sunday school, singing about Jesus, were blown apart by people who claim to be Christians.[15] And this happened in the year 1963, the year that they said in that country would mark a hundred years of good relations between the races.

By 1964—1964 was the year in which three civil rights workers, who were doing nothing other than trying to show Black people in Mississippi how to register and take advantage of their political potential—they were murdered in cold blood. They weren't murdered by some unknown element. They were murdered by an organized group of criminals known as the Ku Klux Klan, which was headed by the sheriff and his deputy and a clergyman. A preacher, a man of the cloth, was responsible for the murder. And when they tell you what was done to the body of that little Black one that they found—all three were murdered, but when they found the three bodies they said that every bone in the body of the Black one was broken, as if these brutes had gone insane while they were beating him to death. This was in 1964.

Now 1965 is here, and you got these same old people, jumping up talking about the "Great Society" now is coming into existence.[16] [*Laughter*] Nineteen sixty-five will be the longest and the hottest and the bloodiest year that has yet been witnessed in the United States. Why? I'm not saying this to advocate violence. [*Laughter*] I'm saying this after a careful analysis of the ingredients—the sociological, political dynamite that exists in every Black community in that country.

Africa is emerging. It's making the Black man in the Western Hemisphere militant. It's making him shift from negative to positive in his image of himself and in his confidence in himself. He sees himself as a new man. He's beginning to identify himself with new forces. Whereas in the past he thought of his problem as one of civil rights— which made it a domestic issue, which kept it confined to the jurisdiction of the United States, a jurisdiction in which he could only seek the aid of white liberals within continental United States—today the Black man in the Western Hemisphere, especially in the United States, is beginning to see where his problem is not one of civil rights, but it is rather one of human rights. And that in the human rights context it becomes an international issue. It ceases to be a Negro problem, it ceases to be an American problem. It becomes a human problem, a problem of human rights, a problem of humanity, a problem for the world.

And by shifting his entire position from civil rights to human rights, he puts it on the world stage and makes it possible where today he no more has to rely on only the white liberals within continental United States to be his supporters. But he brings it onto the world stage and makes it possible for all of our African brothers, our Asian brothers, our Latin American brothers, and those people in Europe, some of whom claim to mean right, also to step into the picture and do whatever is necessary to help us to see that our rights are guaranteed us—not sometime in the long future, but almost immediately.

So the basic difference between the struggle of the Black man in the Western Hemisphere today from the past: he has a new sense of identity; he has a new sense of dignity; he has a new sense of urgency. And above all else, he sees now that he has allies. He sees that the brothers on the African continent, who have emerged and gotten independent states, can see that they have an obligation to the lost brother who went astray and then found himself today in a foreign land. They are obligated. They are just as obligated to the brother who's gone away as they are to the brother who's still at home.

And just as you see the oppressed people all over the world today getting together, the Black people in the West are also seeing that they are oppressed. Instead of just calling themselves an oppressed minority in the States, they are part of the oppressed masses of people all over the world today who are crying out for action against the common oppressor.

Thank you. [*Applause*]

See for yourself,
listen for yourself,
think for yourself

The American system
of exploitation
and oppression

See for yourself, listen for yourself, think for yourself

A DISCUSSION WITH YOUNG CIVIL RIGHTS FIGHTERS
FROM MISSISSIPPI, JANUARY 1, 1965[17]

The speech that follows was given at the Hotel Theresa in Harlem to a group of Black high school students from McComb, Mississippi. Thirty-seven of these young civil rights fighters had come to New York on an eight-day study trip sponsored by the Student Nonviolent Coordinating Committee (SNCC).

McComb was where SNCC had begun its voter registration project and held Mississippi's first sit-in in 1961. A center of the 1964 voter registration and desegregation campaigns, McComb was also the site of more than a dozen racist bombings.

I was approached, I think we were at the United Nations, and I met Mrs. Walker, about two or three weeks ago, and she said that a group of students were coming up from McComb, Mississippi, and wanted to know if I would meet with you and speak with you. I told her frankly that it would be the greatest honor that I ever had experienced. Because I have never been in the state of Mississippi, number one—not through any fault of my own, I don't think—but it's been my great desire to either go there or meet someone from there.

To not take too much of your time, I would like to point out a little incident that I was involved in a short while ago that will give you somewhat of an idea of why I am going to say what I am.

I was flying on a plane from Algiers to Geneva about four weeks ago, with two other Americans. Both of them were white—one was a male, the other was a female. And after we had flown together for about forty minutes, the lady turned to me and asked me—she had looked at my briefcase and saw the initials *M* and *X*—and she said, "I would like to ask you a question. What kind of last name could you have that begins with *X?*"

So I told her, "That's it: *X.*"

She was quiet for a little while. For about ten minutes she was quiet. She hadn't been quiet at all up to then, you know. And then finally she turned and she said, "Well, what's your first name?"

I said, "Malcolm."

She was quiet for about ten more minutes. Then she turned and she said, "Well, you're not *Malcolm X?*" [*Laughter*]

But the reason she asked that question was, she had gotten from the press, and from things that she had heard and read, she was looking for something different, or for someone different.

The reason I take time to tell you this is, one of the first things I think young people, especially nowadays, should learn how to do is see for yourself and listen for yourself and think for yourself. Then you can come to an intelligent decision for yourself. But if you form the habit of going by what you hear others say about someone, or going by what others think about someone, instead of going and searching that thing out for yourself and seeing for yourself, you'll be walking west when you think you're going east, and you'll be walking east when you think you're going west. So this generation, especially of our people, have a burden upon themselves, more so than at any other time in history. The most important thing we can learn how to do today is think for ourselves.

It's good to keep wide-open ears and listen to what everybody else has to say, but when you come to make a decision, you have to weigh all of what you've heard on its own, and place it where it belongs, and then come to a decision for yourself. You'll never regret it. But if you form the habit of taking what someone else says about a thing without checking it out for yourself, you'll find that other people will have you hating your own friends and loving your enemies. This is one of the things that our people are beginning to learn today—that it is very important to think out a situation for yourself. If you don't do it, then you'll always be maneuvered into actually—You'll never fight your enemies, but you will find yourself fighting your own self.

I think our people in this country are the best examples of that. Because many of us want to be nonviolent. We talk very loudly, you know, about being nonviolent. Here in Harlem, where there are probably more Black people concentrated than any place else in the world, some talk that nonviolent talk too. And when they stop talking about how nonviolent they are, we find that they aren't nonviolent with each other. At Harlem Hospital, you can go out here on Friday night, which—today is what, Friday? yes—you can go out here to Harlem Hospital, where there are more Black patients in one hospital than any hospital in the world—because there's a concentration of our people here—and find Black people who claim they're nonviolent. But you see them going in there all cut up and shot up and busted up where they got violent with each other.

So my experience has been that in many instances where you find Negroes always talking about being nonviolent, they're not nonviolent with each other, and they're not loving with each other, or patient with each other, or forgiving with each other. Usually, when they say they're nonviolent, they mean they're nonviolent with somebody else. I think you understand what I mean. They are nonviolent with the enemy. A person can come to your home, and if he's white and he wants to heap some kind of brutality upon you, you're nonviolent. Or he can come put a rope around your neck, you're nonviolent. Or he can come to take your father out and put a rope around his neck, you're nonviolent. But now if another Negro just stomps his foot, you'll rumble with him in a minute. Which shows you there's an inconsistency there.

So I myself would go for nonviolence if it was consistent,

if it was intelligent, if everybody was going to be nonviolent, and if we were going to be nonviolent all the time. I'd say, okay, let's get with it, we'll all be nonviolent. But I don't go along—and I'm just telling you how I think—I don't go along with any kind of nonviolence unless everybody's going to be nonviolent. If they make the Ku Klux Klan nonviolent, I'll be nonviolent. If they make the White Citizens' Council nonviolent, I'll be nonviolent.[18] But as long as you've got somebody else not being nonviolent, I don't want anybody coming to me talking any kind of nonviolent talk. I don't think it is fair to tell our people to be nonviolent unless someone is out there making the Klan and the Citizens' Council and these other groups also be nonviolent.

Now I'm not criticizing those here who are nonviolent. I think everybody should do it the way they feel is best, and I congratulate anybody who can be nonviolent in the face of all that kind of action that I read about in that part of the world. But I don't think that in 1965 you will find the upcoming generation of our people, especially those who have been doing some thinking, who will go along with any form of nonviolence unless nonviolence is going to be practiced all the way around.

If the leaders of the nonviolent movement can go into the white community and teach nonviolence, good. I'd go along with that. But as long as I see them teaching nonviolence only in the Black community, then we can't go along with that. We believe in equality, and equality means you have to put the same thing over here that you put over there. And if just Black people alone are going to be the ones who are nonviolent, then it's not fair. We throw ourselves off guard. In fact, we disarm ourselves and make ourselves defenseless.

Now to try and give you a better understanding of our own position, I guess you have to know something about the Black Muslim movement, which is supposed to be a religious movement in this country, which was extremely militant, vocally militant, or militantly vocal. The Black

Muslim movement was supposed to be a religious group. And because it was supposed to be a religious group, it never involved itself in civic matters, so it claimed. And by not getting involved in civic matters, what it did, being militant, it attracted the most militant Negroes, or Afro-Americans, in this country, which it actually did. The Black Muslim movement attracted the most dissatisfied, impatient, and militant Black people in this country.

But when it attracted them, the movement itself, by never involving itself in the real struggle that's confronting Black people in this country, in a sense has gotten maneuvered into a sort of a political and civic vacuum. It was militant, it was vocal, but it never got into the battle itself.

And though it professed to be a religious group, the people from the part of the world whose religion it had adopted didn't recognize them or accept them as a religious group. So it was also in a religious vacuum. It was in a vacuum religiously, by claiming to be a religious group and by having adopted a religion which actually rejected them or wouldn't accept them. So religiously it was in a vacuum. The federal government tried to classify it as a political group, in order to maneuver it into a position where they could label it as seditious, so that they could crush it because they were afraid of its uncompromising, militant characteristics. So for that reason, though it was labeled a political group and never took part in politics, it was in a political vacuum. So the group, the Black Muslim movement itself, actually developed into a sort of a hybrid, a religious hybrid, a political hybrid, a hybrid-type organization.

Getting all of these very militant Black people into it, and then not having a program that would enable them to take an active part in the struggle, it created a lot of dissatisfaction among its members. It polarized into two different factions—one faction that was militantly vocal, and another faction that wanted some action, militant action, uncompromising action. Finally the dissatisfaction developed into a division, the division developed into a split, and many of its members left. Those who left formed what was known as the Muslim Mosque, Inc., which is authentically a religious organization that is affiliated with and recognized by all of the official religious heads in the Muslim world. This was called the Muslim Mosque, Inc., whose offices are here.

But this group, being Afro-American or being Black American, realized that although we were practicing the religion of Islam, still there was a problem confronting our people in this country that had nothing to do with religion and went above and beyond religion. A religious organization couldn't attack that problem according to the magnitude of the problem, the complexity of the problem itself. So those in that group, after analyzing the problem, saw the need, or the necessity, of forming another group that had nothing to do with religion whatsoever. And that group is what's named and is today known as the Organization of Afro-American Unity.

The Organization of Afro-American Unity is a nonreligious group of Black people in this country who believe that the problems confronting our people in this country need to be reanalyzed and a new approach devised toward trying to get a solution. Studying the problem, we recall that prior to 1939 in this country, all of our people— in the North, South, East, and West, no matter how much education we had—were segregated. We were segregated in the North just as much as we were segregated in the South. And even right now, today, there's as much segregation in the North as there is in the South. There's some worse segregation right here in New York City than there is in McComb, Mississippi; but up here they're subtle and tricky and deceitful, and they make you think that you've got it made when you haven't even begun to make it yet.

Prior to 1939 our people were in a very menial position or condition. Most of us were waiters and porters and bellhops and janitors and waitresses and things of that sort. It was not until war was declared in Germany by

Hitler, and America became involved in a manpower shortage in regards to her factories plus her army—it was only then that the Black man in this country was permitted to make a few strides forward. It was never out of some kind of moral enlightenment or moral awareness on the part of Uncle Sam. Uncle Sam only let the Black man take a step forward when he himself had his back to the wall.

In Michigan, where I was brought up at that time, I recall that the best jobs in the city for Blacks were waiters out at the country club. And in those days if you had a job waiting table in the country club, you had it made. Or if you had a job at the State House. Having a job at the State House didn't mean that you were a clerk or something of that sort—you had the shoeshine stand in the State House. Just by being in there where you could be around all these big politicians, that made you a big-shot Negro. You were shining shoes, but you were a big-shot Negro because you were around big-shot white people and you could bend their ear and get up next to them. And ofttimes in those days, you were chosen to be the voice of the Negro community.

Also right at this time, 1939 or '40, '41, they weren't drafting Negroes in the army or the navy. A Negro couldn't join the navy in 1940 or '41 in this country. He couldn't join. They wouldn't take a Black man in the navy. They would take him if they wanted and make him a cook. But he couldn't just go and join the navy. And he couldn't just go—I don't think he could just go and join the army. They weren't drafting him when the war first started.

This is what they thought of you and me in those days. For one thing, they didn't trust us. They feared that if they put us in the army and trained us on how to use rifles and other things, that we might shoot at some targets that they hadn't picked out. And we would have. Any thinking man knows what target to shoot at. And if a man doesn't, if he has to have someone else to choose his target, then he's not thinking for himself—they're doing the thinking for him.

So it was only when the Negro leaders—they had the same type of Negro leaders in those days that we have today—when the Negro leaders saw all the white fellows being drafted and taken into the army and dying on the battlefield, and no Negroes were dying because they weren't being drafted, the Negro leaders came up and said, "We've got to die too. We want to be drafted too, and we demand that you take us in there and let us die for our country too." This is what the Negro leaders said, back in 1940, I remember. A. Philip Randolph was one of the leading Negroes in those days who said it, and he's one of the Big Six right now; and this is why he's one of the Big Six right now.[19]

They started drafting Negro soldiers then, and then they started letting Negroes get into the navy—but not until Hitler and Tojo[20] and the foreign powers were strong enough to bring pressure upon this country, so that it had its back to the wall and it needed us. At that same time, they let us work in factories. Up until that time we couldn't work in the factories. I'm talking about the North as well as the South. And when they let us work in the factories we began—at first when they let us in we could only be janitors. Then, after a year or so passed by, they let us work on machines. We became machinists, got a little skill. And as we got a little more skill, we made a little more money, which enabled us to live in a little better neighborhood. When we lived in a little better neighborhood, we went to a little better school, got a little better education, and could come out and get a little better job. So the cycle was broken somewhat.

But the cycle was not broken because of some kind of sense of moral responsibility on the part of the government. No, the only time that cycle was broken even to a degree was when world pressure was brought to bear upon the United States government and they were forced to look at the Negro—and then they didn't even look at us as human beings, they just put us into their system and let us advance a little bit farther because it served their interests. But they never let us advance a little bit farther because they were interested in our interests, or interested in us as human beings. Any of you who have a knowledge of history, sociology, political science, or the economic development of this country and its race relations, all you have to do is take what I'm telling you and go back and do some research on it and you'll have to admit that this is true.

It was during the time that Hitler and Tojo were able to make war with this country and put pressure upon them that Negroes in this country advanced a little bit. At the end of the war with Germany and Japan, then Joe Stalin and Communist Russia were a threat. And during that period we made a little bit more advances.

Now the point that I'm making is this: Never at any time in the history of our people in this country have we made advances or advancement, or made progress in any way just based upon the internal good will of this country, or based upon the internal activity of this country. We have only made advancement in this country when this country was under pressure from forces above and beyond its control. Because the internal moral consciousness of this country is bankrupt. It hasn't existed since they first brought us over here and made slaves out of us. They trick up on the confirmation and make it appear that they have our good interests at heart. But when you study it, every time, no matter how many steps they take us forward, it's like we're standing on a—what do you call that thing?—a treadmill. The treadmill is moving backwards faster than we're able to go forward in this direction. We're not even standing still—we're walking forward, at the same time we're going backward.

I say that because the Organization of Afro-American Unity, in studying the process of this so-called progress during the past twenty years, realized that the only time the Black man in this country is given any kind of recog-

Previous page: At the offices of the British Broadcasting
Corporation in London, December 2, 1964. • PHOTO: PRESS ASSOCIATION
Above: Speaking at the Great Hall of the University of Ghana,
May 13, 1964. • PHOTO: ALICE WINDOM

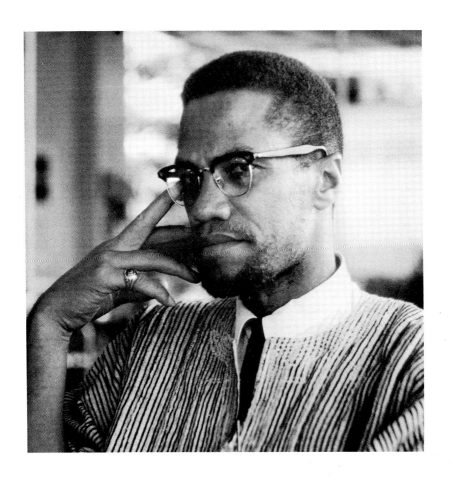

At airport before leaving Ghana, May 17, 1964. •

Entering hall prior to debate at Britain's Oxford University,
December 3, 1964. • PHOTO: OXFORD MAIL

During a trip to Smethwick, England, December 2, 1964. The visit was to show solidarity with the town's Black community, which was the target of a racist attack led by the local Conservative Party member of Parliament. • PHOTO: SYNDICATION INTERNATIONAL

Scenes from a speaking engagement at Tuskegee Institute, a predominantly Black university in Alabama, where Malcolm X addressed several thousand students February 3, 1965.

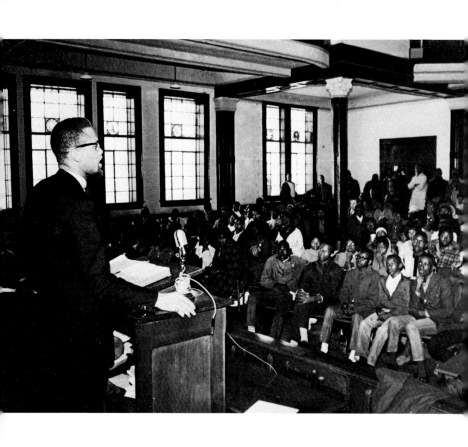

Addressing young civil rights fighters in Selma, Alabama,
February 4, 1965, during struggle over the right to register to vote.

● PHOTO: WIDE WORLD

nition, or shown any kind of favor at all, or even his voice is listened to, is when America is afraid of outside pressure, or when she's afraid of her image abroad. We could see that as long as we sat around and carried on our struggle at a level or in a manner that involved only the good will of the internal forces of this country, we would continue to go backward, there would be no real meaningful changes made. So the Organization of Afro-American Unity saw that it was necessary to expand the problem and the struggle of the Black man in this country until it went above and beyond the jurisdiction of the United States.

For the past fifteen years the struggle of the Black man in this country was labeled as a civil rights struggle, and as such it remained completely within the jurisdiction of the United States. You and I could get no kind of benefits whatsoever other than that which would be forthcoming from Washington, D.C. Which meant, in order for it to be forthcoming from Washington, D.C., all of the congressmen and the senators would have to agree to it.

But the most powerful congressmen and the most powerful senators were from the South. And they were from the South because they had seniority in Washington, D.C. And they had seniority because our people in the South, where they came from, couldn't vote. They didn't have the right to vote.

So when we saw that we were up against a hopeless battle internally, we saw the necessity of getting allies at the world level or from abroad, from all over the world. And so immediately we realized that as long as the struggle was a civil rights struggle, was under the jurisdiction of the United States, we would have no real allies or real support. We decided that the only way to make the problem rise to the level where we could get world support was to take it away from the civil rights label, and put in the human rights label.

It is not an accident that the struggle of the Black man in this country for the past ten or fifteen years has been called a struggle for civil rights. Because as long as you're struggling for civil rights, what you are doing is asking these racist segregationists who control Washington, D.C.—and they control Washington, D.C., they control the federal government through these committees—as long as this thing is a civil rights struggle, you are asking it at a level where your so-called benefactor is actually someone from the worst part of this country. You can only go forward to the degree that they let you.

But when you get involved in a struggle for human rights, it's completely out of the jurisdiction of the United States government. You take it to the United Nations. And any problem that is taken to the United Nations, the United States has no say-so on it whatsoever. Because in the UN she only has one vote, and in the UN the largest bloc of votes is African; the continent of Africa has the largest bloc of votes of any continent on this earth. And the continent of Africa, coupled with the Asian bloc and the Arab bloc, comprises over two-thirds of the UN forces, and they're the dark nations. That's the only court that you can go to today and get your own people, the people who look like you, on your side—the United Nations.

This could have been done fifteen years ago. It could have been done nineteen years ago. But they tricked us. They got ahold of our leaders and used our leaders to lead us right back to their courts, knowing that they control their courts. So the leaders look like they're leading us against an enemy, but when you analyze the struggle that we've been involved in for the past fifteen years, the good or the progress that we've made is actually disgraceful. We should be ashamed to even use the word "progress" in the context of our struggle.

So there has been a move on—and I will conclude in a moment—there has been a move on to keep the Negro thinking in this country that he was making strides in the civil rights field, only for the purpose of distracting him and not letting him know that were he to acquaint himself with the structure of the United Nations and the politics of the United Nations, the aim and the purpose of the United Nations, he could lift his problem into that world body. And he'd have the strongest stick in the world that he could use against the racists in Mississippi.

But one of the arguments against getting you and me to do this has always been that our problem is a domestic problem of the United States. And as such, we should not think to put it at a level where somebody else can come and mess with United States domestic affairs. But you're giving Uncle Sam a break. Uncle Sam's got his hands in the Congo, in Cuba, in South America, in Saigon. Uncle Sam has got his bloody hands in every continent and in everybody else's business on this earth. But at the same time, when it comes to taking forceful action in this country where our rights are concerned, he's always going to tell you and me, "Well, these are states' rights." Or he'll make some kind of off-the-wall alibi that's not a bona fide alibi—not because it's an alibi, but to justify his inactivity where your and my rights are concerned.

We were successful when we realized that we had to bring this to the United Nations. We knew that we had to get support, we had to get world support, and that the most logical part of the world to look in for support is among people who look just like you and me.

I was fortunate to be able to take a tour of the African continent during the summer—the Middle East and Africa. I went to Egypt, then to Arabia, Kuwait, Lebanon, and then to Sudan, Ethiopia, Kenya, Tanganyika, Zanzibar, Nigeria, Ghana, Guinea, Liberia, and Algeria. I found while I was traveling on the African continent—I had already detected it in May—that someone has very shrewdly planted the seeds of division on this continent to make the Africans not show genuine concern with our problem, just as they plant seeds in your and my minds so that we won't show concern with the African problem. They try and make you and me think that we're separate, and the two problems are separate.

When I went back this time and traveled to those different countries, I was fortunate enough to spend an hour and a half with Nasser in Egypt, which is a North African country; and three hours with President Nyerere in Tanganyika, which has now become Tanzania, which is an East African country; and with Prime Minister Obote, Milton Obote, in Uganda, which is also an East African country; and with Jomo Kenyatta in Kenya, which is another East African country; and with President Azikiwe in Nigeria, President Nkrumah in Ghana, and President Sékou Touré in Guinea.

I found that in every one of these African countries, the head of state is genuinely concerned with the problem of the Black man in this country, but many of them thought that if they opened their mouths and voiced concern, that they would be insulted by the American Negro leaders. Because one head of state in Asia voiced his support of the civil rights struggle and a couple of the Big Six had the audacity to slap his face and say they weren't interested in that kind of help—which in my opinion is asinine.[21] So that the African leaders only had to be convinced that if they took an open stand at the governmental level and showed interest in the problem of Black people in this country, that they wouldn't be rebuffed.

And today you'll find in the United Nations—and it's not an accident—that every time the Congo question or anything on the African continent is being debated in the Security Council, they couple it with what's going on, or what is happening to you and me, in Mississippi and Alabama and these other places. In my opinion, the greatest accomplishment that was made in the struggle of the Black man in America in 1964 toward some kind of real progress was the successful linking together of our problem with the African problem, or making our problem a world problem. Because now, whenever anything happens to you in Mississippi, it's not a case of just somebody in Alabama getting indignant, or somebody in New York getting indignant. Whatever happens in Mississippi today, with the attention of the African nations drawn toward Mississippi at a governmental level, then the same repercussions that you see all over the world when an imperialist or foreign power interferes in some section of Africa, you see repercussions, you see the embassies being bombed and burned and overturned. Nowadays, when something happens to Black people in Mississippi, you will see the same repercussions all over the world.

I wanted to point this out to you, because it is important for you to know that when you're in Mississippi you're not alone. But as long as you think you're alone, then you take a stand as if you're a minority or as if you're out-numbered, and that kind of stand will never enable you to win a battle. You've got to know that you've got as much power on your side as that Ku Klux Klan has on its side. And when you know that you've got just as much power on your side as the Klan has on its side, you'll talk the same kind of language with that Klan as that Klan is talking with you.

I'll say one more thing, and then I'll conclude.

When I say the same kind of language, I should explain what I mean. See, you can never get good relations with anybody that you can't communicate with. You can never have good relations with anybody that doesn't under-stand you. There has to be an understanding. Under-standing is brought about through dialogue. Dialogue is communication of ideas. This can only be done in a lan-guage, a common language. You can never talk French to somebody who speaks only German and think you're com-municating. Neither of them—they don't get the point. You have to be able to speak a man's language in order to make him get the point.

Now, you've lived in Mississippi long enough to know what the language of the Ku Klux Klan is. They only know one language. If you come up with another lan-guage, you don't communicate. You've got to be able to speak the same language they speak, whether you're in Mississippi, New York City, or Alabama, or California, or anywhere else. When you develop or mature to the point where you can speak another man's language on his level, that man gets the point. That's the only time he gets the point. You can't talk peace to a person who doesn't know what peace means. You can't talk love to a person who doesn't know what love means. And you can't talk any form of nonviolence to a person who doesn't believe in nonviolence. Why, you're wasting your time.

So I think in 1965—whether you like it, or I like it, or we like it, or they like it, or not—you will see that there is a generation of Black people born in this country who become mature to the point where they feel that they have no more business being asked to take a peaceful approach than anybody else takes, unless everybody's going to take a peaceful approach.

So we here in the Organization of Afro-American Unity, we're with the struggle in Mississippi 1,000 percent. We're with the efforts to register our people in Mississippi to vote 1,000 percent. But we do not go along with anybody telling us to help nonviolently. We think if the government says that Negroes have a right to vote, and then when Negroes go out to vote some kind of Ku Klux Klan is going to put them in the river, and the government doesn't do anything about it, it's time for us to organize and band together and equip ourselves and qualify ourselves to protect ourselves. [*Applause*] And once you can protect yourself, you don't have to worry about being hurt. That's it. [*Applause*]

DISCUSSION PERIOD

So we're going to have a few minutes now for you to ask questions on all that that has been said, and all that that hasn't been said.

Yes, sir.

QUESTIONER: Could you please say something on the Freedom Democratic Party?

MALCOLM X: Yes. We support the Freedom Democratic

Party. We have a statement that we're making in support.
We had a rally last Sunday night—no, a week ago Sunday
night, to which we invited Mrs. Hamer. She spoke and
explained the position of the Mississippi Freedom Democratic Party, and we support it.[22] We know that in Washington—

To give you an example of why we support this, it has as
much effect on New York City as it does in Mississippi.

But by the same token, I must point out that those who
are depriving you of your rights in Mississippi aren't all
in Mississippi. You got these New York Democrats [who]
are just as much responsible. The mayor of this city is a
Democrat. The senator, you've heard of him, Robert Kennedy, he's a Democrat. The president of the country is a
Democrat. The vice president is a Democrat. Now don't
you tell me anything about a Democrat in Mississippi
who is depriving you of your rights, when the power of the
Democratic Party is in Washington, D.C., and in New
York City, and in Chicago, and some of these northern
cities.

When you put the power or the pressure upon these
people who walk around here posing as liberals—

In New York City Negroes can already vote. When you
make known in the city of New York the position of the
Mississippi Freedom Democratic Party, and why it was
necessary to form that party, and what that party is
trying to do toward ousting these illegal representatives
from Mississippi, then the Negroes in New York City
know what it's all about. We want to know, where does
[Mayor Robert] Wagner stand, since he's one of the most
powerful and influential leaders of the Democratic Party
in the United States. And we want to know where the
senator, Robert Kennedy, stands, since he's also one of the
most powerful and influential leaders of the Democratic
Party in the United States. And we've got a Negro [J.
Raymond Jones] who's the assistant to the mayor in this
city. We want to know where he stands. Plus you got
Lyndon B. Johnson and Hubert Humphrey, who professes

to drool at the mouth over Negroes, to let you know where they stand before January 4.[23]

When you get that kind of action off some of these northern Democrats, then you'll get some action in Mississippi. You don't have to worry about that man in Mississippi. The power of the Democratic Party are these people up here who hold all the power in the North.

So we're with you, but we want to go all the way.

See, as a Muslim, I don't get my religion involved in my politics, because they clash. They don't clash, but when you go into something as a Muslim, you've got a whole lot of Negroes who are Christians, who aren't broad-minded enough, so you get into a religious argument, and it doesn't pay.

So I don't enter into this struggle as a Muslim, inasmuch as I enter into it as a member of the Organization of Afro-American Unity. And the stand that the Organization of Afro-American Unity takes is that we get into it without compromising.

You compromise when you're wrong. You don't have to compromise when you're right. Why, you're right. They're not giving you something. This is yours. If you were born in this country, nobody's doing you any favor when they let you vote or when they let you register. They're only recognizing you as a human being and recognizing your right as a human being to exercise your right as a citizen. So they're not doing you any favors.

As long as you approach this thing like somebody has done you a favor, or that you're dealing with a friend, you never can fight that fight. Because when they deal with you, they're not dealing with you like they're dealing with a friend. They look at you like you're an enemy. Now you have to look at them just as if they're an enemy. And once you know what it is you're dealing with, you can deal with that thing. But you can't deal with them with love. Why, man, if there was any love with them, if there was any love in them, you wouldn't have any fight in Mississippi. There's no love there. You have to realize that there's no love there, and then you don't be looking for it, and go ahead and fight them.

When you go to vote or register and someone gets in your way, you're supposed to answer them in the same way that they answer you. When you answer them that way, you get a little dialogue. And if you don't have enough of them down there to do it, we'll come down there and help you do it. Because we are tired of this old runaround that our people have been given in this country.

For a long time they accused me of not getting involved in politics. They should've been glad I didn't get involved in politics, because anything I get in, I'm in it all the way. Now if they say that we don't take part in the Mississippi struggle, we will organize brothers here in New York who know how to handle these kinds of affairs, and they'll slip into Mississippi like Jesus slipped into Jerusalem. [*Laughter and applause*]

This doesn't mean that we're against white people, but we sure are against the Ku Klux Klan and the White Citizens' Councils. Anything that looks like it's against us, we're against it.

Excuse me for raising my voice, but this thing, you know, it gets me upset. Even being involved in a discussion in a country that's supposed to be a democracy. Imagine that, in a country that's supposed to be a democracy, supposed to be for freedom and all of that kind of stuff that they tell you when they want to draft you and put you in the army and send you to Saigon to fight for them. And then you've got to turn around and all night long discuss how you're going to just get a right to register and vote without being murdered. Why, that's the most hypocritical governmental half-truth that has ever been invented since the world was the world.

Yes, ma'am.

QUESTIONER: The question I have is what does the Afro-American Unity do?

MALCOLM X: First, Afro-American means us.

QUESTIONER: I know what it means, I just want to know: What does it do?

MALCOLM X: How do you mean?

QUESTIONER: What kind of struggles, what does it do?

MALCOLM X: Well, first, it was patterned after the OAU. The OAU is the Organization of African Unity. And the reason we patterned our organization after theirs was they had trouble on the African continent similar to ours. Meaning that there were many independent countries that were so divided against each other that they couldn't come together in a united effort and resolve any of their problems. So some of the more mature African politicians were able to work behind the scenes and get a common understanding, out of which materialized the Organization of African Unity, the purpose of which was to get all African leaders to see the necessity of de-emphasizing their areas of disagreement and emphasizing their areas of agreement, where they had common interests.

This led to the Organization of African Unity being formed, and today they work together in unity and harmony, although there are diverse philosophies, diverse personalities. All of these differences exist; still they can unite together for a common objective.

So studying their problems, and seeing that their problems were similar to ours, we formed ours after the letter and spirit of that OAU, only with an OAAU.[24]

Our first objective is—our first step was to find an area of agreement among Afro-Americans. We found that you have the nationalists, you have the civil rights groups, you have all these diverse elements in the Black community. Some want separation, some want integration; some want this, some want that. So how are you going to find something that they all agree upon? You won't find the nationalists agree on civil rights, because they think it's a farce. You won't find the nationalists agree on integration, because they think it's a farce. They haven't seen anyplace where it has ever materialized. It's only a word, something that's played around, kicked around.

So we had to find something that both the nationalists and the integrationists would agree upon. And we found that all of them would agree on the necessity of our people in this country being respected and recognized as human beings. So instead of launching our struggle at the civil rights level that would cause a whole lot of argument, we launched it at the human rights level. And we know that anybody that's for civil rights has got to be for human rights, whether you're an integrationist or a separationist or what you are; you still have to be for human rights.

So our first platform was that we recognized the right of the Black man in the Western Hemisphere to exercise his right as a human being. Rights that he was born with, rights that no government has the power to give him. God makes you a human being, and God is the one who gives you your human rights, not a government, or some senators, or a judge, or some representatives. And so this is our stand. We are human beings, and our fight is to see that every Black man, woman, and child in this country is respected and recognized as a human being.

Our method is: any means necessary. That's our motto. We're not restricted to this, or confined to that. We reserve the right to use any means necessary to protect our humanity, or to make the world see that they respect us as human beings. Any means necessary.

When I say that, I don't mean anything illegal. The government— You're being treated criminally. The criminal is the one who's illegal. The one who's responsible for these criminal conditions, he's a criminal, he's illegal. And whatever you've got to do to stop this crime from being committed against you, as far as I'm concerned you're not illegal.

So that's our first step at the international level. And politically, we devise and support any program that's designed to give the Black man in this country an opportunity to participate as a citizen, a free citizen, in this political system and in this society. We will involve ourselves in programs of our own, or in anyone else's programs, as long as it doesn't involve any kind of compromise in its approach to getting our people in this country the rights to register and to vote in whichever direction they desire to.

QUESTIONER: [*Inaudible*]

MALCOLM X: The voter registration?

QUESTIONER: How important is it?

MALCOLM X: We ourselves have our own voter registration drive in the areas where we are, plus we work with other civil rights groups who also have voter registration drives.

QUESTIONER: [*Inaudible*]

MALCOLM X: No. Not as yet. . . . [*Inaudible*] keep it, what's the word, keep it to ourselves, we would keep it confidential. We will never let you know how many members we have.

QUESTIONER: I'm not asking that.

MALCOLM X: I learned that. I'm giving you some light without you asking. That's one thing I learned in the Black Muslim movement that I found most important: never let anybody know what they're dealing with—its size, its strength, its nothing. The reason for that is, I found, if you're in the jungle or in the woods and you hear something rustling in the bush, you don't know what kind of gun to reach for until you know what's making that noise. Because you might pull out a rabbit gun for an elephant, or you might pull out an elephant gun for a rabbit, and you look foolish either way. It's not good to ever let too much of what you are come out above the ground. The most important part of the tree is the roots, and the roots always remain beneath the ground. That's where the tree gets its life. And the tree dies only when you put those roots up where the light is and it dries up.

So our membership—its nature, its caliber, its content, all of that—we keep it to ourselves. But you see here and there, wherever you find dissatisfied Negroes, if they're not our blood brothers, they're at least some relatives, some relation. If we're not blood brothers, we're at least related.

Any more?

QUESTIONER: We obviously can't say—

MALCOLM X: You from Mississippi too?

QUESTIONER: No, I'm not.

MALCOLM X: I didn't think so. [*Laughter*] Keep on asking.

QUESTIONER: Obviously you can't say what you do. I just was wondering what kind of—

MALCOLM X: It's not a case of I can't say what we do. I told you that we involve ourselves in our own programs to get our people registered, as registered voters in this area and wherever else we are. And we work with any other group that's trying to get our people registered so that they can vote. This is in this political area or in the area of politics. Now what else did you want to know, since you don't seem to be satisfied?

QUESTIONER: Well, maybe. Do you think—

MALCOLM X: No, if that's not clear, ask me. I mean, if I didn't clarify your question, go ahead and dig into it a little deeper.

QUESTIONER: No, I think that man from the other . . . [*Inaudible*] don't vote either, which makes it look like—

MALCOLM X: This is true, which shows you that the reluctance on the part of the Negro to vote isn't always because they don't have the right to. The political history of our people in this country has been that usually you have political machines in most states and in most cities. And they select, as a rule, not Black people to run in the Black community who are intellectually capable to deal with politics as it is, but puppets that serve as their mouthpiece to control the politics of the community. The Black people in Harlem have witnessed this thing year in and year out and have seen how the politics of Harlem and other Negro communities have been pretty much controlled from outside.

So it's not that they're politically lethargic or dead, but they purposely have abstained. But when you give them something to point toward, or vote for, you'll find that they'll be just as active as they've been inactive.

It's the purpose of the OAAU to work among that element of inactive Black people, who have been politically inactive in this area. We intend to charge them and get them active out here, so that we can get a little action. Because those are the real activists. Those who haven't been involved in politics actively are the ones who get involved in physical action. They have not seen anything that's good be made to materialize through politics in the past, so they didn't resort to politics. They resorted to things physical, to methods physical, if you understand what I mean.

What we intend to do is try and harness their energy by giving them an understanding of politics, first. Because we don't think that anybody should get us registered as voters and not at the same time give us some education in regards to politics. We don't think that a voter registration program on its own is sufficient. But in line with any voter registration program among Negroes, there must be a voter education program to make our people enlightened in regards to the science of politics, so that they will know what politics is supposed to produce and what the politician is supposed to produce, what his responsibilities are. And then we can't be exploited.

But if you just get Negroes out here and register them, then what you're going to have are more Negroes whose political energy can be exploited by the big city political machines. We don't think that that will ever solve our problems. There has to be voter education as well as voter registration. Most of the Negro politicians don't want this, because those who have been politicians haven't really been trying to solve our problems, inasmuch as they've been getting the handouts from the machine for keeping us in check. When the people realize that, the people wake up.

One of the reasons, if I may add, that Negroes haven't been actively involved in politics is, when the Negro leader—when Negroes go out to try and make other Negroes get registered to vote, they have the wrong motives, usually—especially the politicians. The young students who are doing it today are a little different. But the politician, when he tries to get you registered to vote, he's not interested in making you enlightened so you can vote. He wants you to stay in the dark but register. Then maybe you'll vote for him, or vote for his party, or vote for what he's got going for him. He's not even interested in your condition. And this is why you find Negroes in Harlem haven't gotten involved.

But don't think that they can't get involved. You can get as many Negroes interested politically in Harlem overnight, but you've got to give him something, give him something that he will see will materialize. And I think that our people in this area are ready.

QUESTIONER: [*Inaudible*]

MALCOLM X: Well, there wouldn't have to be necessarily any particular party to make them have something to look forward to, especially up around here. It takes something else to make these people in Harlem feel that they have something to look forward to.

QUESTIONER: [*Inaudible, asks about "political pressure" in Harlem*]

MALCOLM X: No, not particularly. Although, the only real power in this government is politics—and money. The only thing that people recognize is power and money. Power—that's all they recognize. That's why I say, in Mississippi you can love all you want. They don't recognize love, they recognize power. Power. You can love, look how long you've been loving, that's proof of it. You've been loving them like a blind—

QUESTIONER: It's not love—

MALCOLM X: Yeah, I understand, but— [*Laughter*]

QUESTIONER: Don't let love . . . [*Inaudible*]

MALCOLM X: Brother, I will read the breakdown. You know, in various counties [in Mississippi] now, you got more Negroes than you got whites. Negroes outnumber the whites. And you see, freedom comes only two ways. There's only two ways that a person gets freedom: either by the ballot or by bullets.

QUESTIONER: [*Inaudible, asks about "the riot you had here"*]

MALCOLM X: In Harlem?

QUESTIONER: Yes.

MALCOLM X: It wasn't a riot. That was a pogrom. You know what a pogrom is? How do you say that? Pogrom. Pogrom is what it was. Pogrom. That wasn't any riot, that was a pogrom. That was the police heaping brutality upon the people of the area. It was a set-up.

QUESTIONER: [*Inaudible*] . . . Could I ask you, what was actually accomplished by this so-called riot?

MALCOLM X: It wasn't a riot. There was a rumor passed on to us in May that the police in New York during the summer were going to try and provoke trouble, so that they could step in and crush the organizing and growth of militant groups that they were afraid, if they were allowed to grow, would get to the size that they could never be controlled.

If you study the characteristics of that so-called riot, every action on the part of the police in Harlem was designed to draw out groups that they felt were equipped and ready to do this thing. The tactics that the police used were designed to draw fire back. They were firing guns at people who didn't have guns. But they were firing to get somebody to fight, to shoot back. The police know you got just as many guns in Harlem as there are in Saigon right now. But none of the groups in Harlem that were equipped and qualified to strike back got involved. None of them got involved.

But the whole thing was set up to try and get them involved, so that they could be crushed while they were still in their embryonic, so-called embryonic stage. As you said, it goes beyond the Mississippi situation. But all of our problems are the same: wrong color.

QUESTIONER: [*Inaudible*]

MALCOLM X: Whether it was the COFO?[25]

QUESTIONER: Right.

MALCOLM X: Any program that's designed to get our people registered is good, especially in Mississippi. Because our people in Mississippi outnumber—there's a greater percentage of our people in the state of Mississippi than there is, probably, in any other state. If the people in Mississippi did have voting rights, what's his name—[Sen. James] Eastland—wouldn't be in Washington, D.C. None of those powerful senators and congressmen who control the committees in Washington, D.C., would be there.

So any effort on the part of any group that gets our people in the state of Mississippi registered, that's good. But my only criticism is sending people on the front lines against well-armed enemies and telling them, "Don't fight." Why, that's insane. I can't go along with that. No.

When those three brothers were murdered down there, it was a drag, it's been a drag on the part of the civil rights groups, the way they've just taken that thing so easy. Hardly nothing has happened. They're telling everybody to be patient, be loving and long-suffering when the whole world is on your side. If you went on the rampage in Mississippi, wouldn't nobody hold it against you. Because the whole world knows that the people down there are the worst things on this earth.

So we go for the operation, but we don't go for sending anybody to a front line and telling them, don't protect themselves. No. Then, after one of your soldiers gets killed, everybody says, well, you're supposed to keep on loving anyway? No, I can't go along with that.

That's what split the Muslim movement. That's what caused the Black Muslim movement to be split. Some of our brothers got hurt and nothing was done about it. Those of us who wanted to do something about it were kept from doing something about it. So we split.[26]

No, I don't go along with any kind of action that ties up my hands and then put me in the ring with Sonny Liston or Cassius Clay. [*Laughter*] No, don't tie my hands, unless you're going to tie up their hands too. Then it's fair.

You don't see the white man sending his people to war somewhere and tying up their hands. No, and if those two hadn't been white, you wouldn't even have known that that happened in Mississippi, because they kill Negroes in Mississippi every day. Ever since we've been here.

I was over in Africa, brother, while all that was going on. And I read about it and I know that it tore the Africans up. Tore 'em up. Why, if you had thrown bombs right and left in Mississippi, you'd have had the world on your side.

I'm not telling you to throw bombs. I'm just telling you what would happen. [*Laughter*] If I told you that, if somebody started throwing bombs around here tomorrow, they'd blame me, put the blame on me. They would never give me credit, but they'd put the blame on me.

Only from Mississippi. Questions. Are you from Mississippi? Are there any other questions?

I hope that you don't think that I'm trying to incite you. But look here, just look at yourselves. Some of you all are teenagers, students. Now how do you think I feel—and I belong to a generation ahead of you—how do you think I feel having to tell you, "We, my generation, sat around like a knot on the wall while the whole world was actually fighting for what were its human rights"—and you've got to be born into a society where you still have that same fight. What did we do, who preceded you? I'll tell what we did: nothing. And don't you make the same mistake we made.

You tell me why a Black man in this society has to wait on the Supreme Court and a white man doesn't have to wait on the Supreme Court. Yet both of them are men.

You tell me why the Congress and the Senate have got to make a Black man a human being, and the same Congress and Senate don't have to make a white man a human being, if they're both men.

You tell why you need a presidential proclamation to

get respect and recognition, and a white man doesn't need it, if we're both men.

I'll tell you why: we're not both men.

A man will die and fight for what is his right. And if he doesn't, if he's not ready to fight and die for what is his right, he's not a man. That's the only way you can look at it. And when you begin to look like you're going to . . . [*Inaudible*] you get what belongs to a man.

But as long as you sit around here waiting on some court that is headed by a Ku Klux Klan judge, or waiting on a Senate that's controlled by a Ku Klux Klan senator, or a Congress that's controlled by a White Citizens' Council congressman, or a White House that's got just as much Klan influence in it as any other part of the country, why, no, you'll never be respected as a human being.

I must say this: I was in Africa, I was in Kenya. Five years ago, one of the men in Africa who had the worst image was Kenyatta. They tried to make you and me think that Kenyatta, Jomo Kenyatta, was a monster. I met Kenyatta. I flew from Tanganyika to Zanzibar to Kenya with Kenyatta, and everybody respects him. He's known there as the father of the country. The white man respects him and the Black man respects him. Five years ago they said he was a leader of the Mau Mau.[27] And they tried to make him appear to be a monster. As long as he didn't have his own independence, he was a monster.

But today Kenyatta is so highly respected it's not an accident that when the brothers in Stanleyville had all these hostages in the Congo, and they wanted to try and save them, who did they choose to moderate the conference that took place between Ambassador Atwood and Tom Kanza in Nairobi? Jomo Kenyatta. The same man that this government and this society was labeling as a monster five years ago, now they turn to him when statesmanship is needed. He had a negative image five years ago because he wouldn't compromise. He was bringing freedom to his people by any means necessary. Now that his people have gotten their freedom, he's respected.

And this is the only way you'll get it. You get freedom by not being confined. You get freedom by letting your enemy know that you'll do anything to get your freedom. You'll get it. It's the only way you'll get it. Then, when you get that kind of attitude, they'll label you as a "crazy Negro," or they'll call you a "crazy nigger"—they don't say Negro. They say, "That nigger's crazy." Or they'll call you an extremist or they'll call you a subversive, or seditious, or a Red, or a radical. But when you stay radical long enough, and get enough people to be just like you, you'll get your freedom. Then, after you get your freedom, they'll talk about what a great person you are, just like they do with Kenyatta. So if Lumumba had lived long enough and consolidated the Congo, they'd talk about him like a great person, because he'd be free and independent.

So don't you run around here trying to make friends with somebody who's depriving you of your rights. They're not your friends. No, they're your enemies. Treat them like that and fight them, and you'll get your freedom. And after you get your freedom, your enemy will respect you. [*Applause*] He *will* respect you.

I say that with no hate. I have no hate in me. I have no hate at all. I don't have any hate. But I've got some sense. [*Laughter*] I think I've got some sense. I'm not going to let somebody who hates me tell me to love him. I'm not that way-out. And you, young as you are, and because you start thinking, you're not going to do it either. The only time you're going to get in that kind of bag is if somebody puts you in there, somebody else, who doesn't have your welfare at heart.

[*Inaudible comment from audience*]

[*Malcolm laughs*] Ah yes, I'm going to explain it. I'm just going to take five more minutes, because Sharon Jackson reminded me of something which I think is very important. It's why at the beginning I mentioned, when I was on this plane, how I rode right next to this man and woman for an hour, and they didn't have the slightest idea who I was, because they were looking for somebody with horns. Usually white people think anybody who is not going to be cool and calm under their extreme brutality has got horns. So this is done by image making. People who make images use images to make you hate their enemies and love your own. No: hate their friends and love their enemies. They use images to do this.

One place they've done it is in the Congo. The Congo is where they told me and you we came from. All my life, when I was a little boy, they said we came out of Africa, and they made believe we came out of the Congo, because that was supposed to be the most savage part of Africa. So you know, we're probably more closely related to the brothers in the Congo than anybody else. And when you hear them talking about cannibals, they're talking about our cousins, about our brothers, you know. If you really want to believe it. But they aren't any more cannibalistic in the Congo than they are in the downtown, there in the Village. There's some real cannibals down there in the Village. [*Laughter*] They'll be eating up anything, you know. [*Laughter*]

In this country what they try and make it appear is that the people in the Congo are savages. And they do this very skillfully in order to justify their being over there. Now when I was in Tanganyika, Dar es Salaam—I think it was in October—some American Negroes, Afro-Americans who live in Dar es Salaam, came to me and told me about this Congolese who was cussing them out. And I asked them, why . . . [*Gap in tape*]

. . . African village. Now you know a village has no air force. A village has no defense against bombs that are being dropped on it. And the pilot in the plane can't tell who the bomb is being dropped upon. It's just being dropped on a village.

So here you have American airplanes being flown by what they call "anti-Castro Cuban, American-trained pilots." Now you see how slick they are. The reason they say "American-trained pilots" is to make you automatically side with them, because they are American-trained. The reason they say they are anti-Castro Cuban pilots is because Castro's already a monster, and if somebody links these people, that they're against Castro, then whoever else they're against, it's all right. It's what you call a journalistic, psychological trick on your mind.

So now you have airplanes that are dropping bombs on Black women, Black children, and Black babies, blowing them to bits in the Congo. They justify it by making it appear to be a humanitarian project. And they get big Negroes in this country to talk to you and tell you that America is justified in doing it. You show me a big Negro and usually he's their big Negro. And his job is to make you and me think that no matter how much atrocity they are committing, that they are right. And they do it with these tricks.

How can you justify dropping a bomb on a village—not a civilization that has all the weapons of warfare, but a village? You don't need to drop a bomb on a village that doesn't even have rifles in it. But it shows you their complete lack of concern for life when that life is clothed in a black skin.

To show you again how merciless they are. They take Tshombe. Tshombe is a Black man, but he's a murderer. He murdered this man called Patrice Lumumba, in cold blood. And this government took Tshombe away from Spain.[28] And this government did do it, because I know people who can tell you how certain high members of this country's State Department got on board a plane with a certain African leader and flew all the way almost to his country, trying to get this African leader to use his influence on other African leaders to make Tshombe acceptable to the people of the African continent. And this happened almost a year before they brought Tshombe back down—to show you what a plot, what a conspiracy that they're involved in.

And here Tshombe is a killer, a murderer—of Patrice Lumumba. They put him over the government in

Léopoldville, and then they used the press to give him an image of acceptability by saying he's the only one that can restore peace to the Congo. Imagine this, he's a murderer. It's like saying Jesse James is the only one can run the bank. Therefore you should let Jesse James run the bank; and the only reason the bank is in trouble is because Jesse James already was in the bank. [*Laughter*]

So just to go one step farther. They take Tshombe and give him enough money to go to South Africa and bring white mercenaries, hired killers, in to fight for him. A mercenary is someone who kills for pay. He doesn't kill because he's patriotic. He doesn't kill because he's loyal. He kills anything in sight for pay, and this is what America is using your tax dollars to support: a Black murderer who hires white murderers to shoot down his own people. Because America knows if she went in and did it, the world wouldn't go along with her.

And then, when these white murderers are heaping so much butchery upon the people in the Oriental province of the Congo, the brothers in the Oriental province are forced to start using some of the methods to keep these white mercenaries and white hired killers from wiping them out. So they shoot hostages. The only reason they held hostages was to keep America's mercenaries from dropping bombs on them. It's the only thing they could do. They held the hostages not because they were cannibals. And they didn't eat people like they're trying to say in the newspapers. Why would they wait to this late date to eat some white meat, when they been over there all those years? And they went in there at a time when they were probably more tasty than they are in times like this. [*Malcolm laughs*]

At the time the hostages were being held, the American government—rather the Congolese government from Stanleyville—sent an emissary, Tom Kanza, their foreign minister, to Kenya, and he was negotiating with Atwood, the ambassador to Kenya from America, at a meeting which Kenyatta was mediating. And at the time that this

was going on, it was then that America dropped the paratroopers in Stanleyville. At no time did the Africans or the
Congolese in any way harm any white hostages until
those paratroopers were dropped. And I think it's America that harmed more than one. If they were savages,
there wouldn't have been a white hostage seen. How are
you going to come out of the sky and save some hostages
that are already in my hands, when I've got some machine guns? No. If you save some, it means that I'm
human and I treated them in a humane way, because I
didn't wipe them all out when I see your airplane coming.

So this old stuff you hear about the government trying
to make you think that their being in the Congo is something humanitarian—it's the most criminal operation
that has ever been carried on by a so-called civilized
government since history was recorded!

The United States was the one responsible there. And
you will find that she will suffer over there, because the
only way she can hold Tshombe in power is to send in
more white troops. The Black troops don't fight for
Tshombe. He needs white troops. And there are too many
Black troops fighting against those white troops for them
to win, for the white ones to win, which means more
whites will have to be added to it and added to it and
added to it.

And first thing you know they'll be hung up in the same
kind of situation that they got themselves bogged down in
in South Vietnam right now. Because all the African nations combined will fight there in the Congo. You don't
need a whole lot of heavy war machinery to fight a war
nowadays. All you need is some darkness and a little
lighting equipment. [*Laughter*] That equalizes things.

We got about three more minutes. Three more minutes.

Well, I want to thank all of you for taking the time to
come to Harlem and especially here. I hope that you have
gotten a better understanding of us. I put it to you just as
plain as I know how to put it; there's no interpretation
necessary. And I want you to know that we're not in any

way trying to advocate any kind of indiscriminate, unintelligent action. But we will go along with you in any kind of intelligent action that you are involved in to protect the lives and property of our people in this country. Any kind of action that you're ever involved in that's designed to protect the lives and the property of our mistreated people in this country, we're with you 1,000 percent. And if you don't feel that you are qualified to do it, we have some brothers who will slip in, as I said earlier, and help train you and show you how to equip yourself in such a manner to deal with these people who need to be dealt with.

And before you dismiss, let me see one of those. . . . [*Inaudible*] I would like to read you this—it's brief—before you leave. It says:

"We applaud the efforts of James Farmer and the other civil rights groups to block the seating of the five illegal representatives from Mississippi when Congress convenes on January 4. We are pleased to see that Mr. Farmer and his civil rights colleagues are so dead earnest in backing the election challenges that have been initiated by the Mississippi Freedom Democratic Party. As chairman of the Organization of Afro-American Unity, I want to state emphatically that we support all uncompromising efforts made by all well-meaning people to unseat the illegal representatives from the state of Mississippi and any other area where our people are denied the right to vote simply because they have been born with dark skin.

"We also insist that since over 97 percent of the Black Americans supported Lyndon B. Johnson, Hubert Humphrey, Robert Kennedy, and the Democratic Party in the recent elections, which is the most overwhelming support given by any minority group to one party and its candidates, I am challenging Lyndon B. Johnson, Hubert Humphrey, and Robert Kennedy, to declare exactly where they stand on the seating of these illegal representatives from Mississippi before January 4."

And they *should* state their case.

"We applaud the lead that has been taken by New York representative William Fitts Ryan in blocking the seating of these Mississippi congressmen, and the firm stand taken at his side by Adam Clayton Powell.[29] Since Mayor Wagner will be in Harlem later this year to obtain the political support of our people in order to remain in City Hall, I challenge Mayor Wagner and his chief assistant, J. Jones, also to let nearly one and a half million Black Americans in New York City know where they stand on the plan to seat illegal representatives before January 4.

"I, for one, along with some friends, plan to be in Washington on January 4 as an observer. We wish to witness and record the stand taken by the so-called liberals, who are seekers of our people's political support at poll time, for we plan to be 100 percent active in all political areas from 1965 onward." [*Applause*]

So I thank you and I hope to see you in Mississippi myself in January.[30] Thank you. [*Applause*]

The American system of exploitation and oppression

INTERVIEW WITH THE 'YOUNG SOCIALIST,' JANUARY 18, 1965

The following interview was given to Jack Barnes and Barry Sheppard, leaders of the Young Socialist Alliance (YSA). Malcolm X read and approved the final text, which appeared in the March-April 1965 issue of the *Young Socialist.*

YOUNG SOCIALIST: What image of you has been projected by the press?

MALCOLM X: Well, the press has purposely and skillfully projected me in the image of a racist, a race supremacist, and an extremist.

YOUNG SOCIALIST: What's wrong with this image? What do you really stand for?

MALCOLM X: First, I'm not a racist. I'm against every form of racism and segregation, every form of discrimination. I believe in human beings, and that all human beings should be respected as such, regardless of their color.

YOUNG SOCIALIST: Why did you break with the Black Muslims?

MALCOLM X: I didn't break, there was a split. The split came about primarily because they put me out, and they put me out because of my uncompromising approach to problems I thought should be solved and the movement could solve.

I felt the movement was dragging its feet in many areas. It didn't involve itself in the civil or civic or political struggles our people were confronted by. All it did was stress the importance of moral reformation—don't drink, don't smoke, don't permit fornication and adultery. When I found that the hierarchy itself wasn't practicing what it preached, it was clear that this part of its program was bankrupt.[31]

So the only way it could function and be meaningful in the community was to take part in the political and economic facets of the Negro struggle. And the organization wouldn't do that because the stand it would have to take would have been too militant, uncompromising, and activist, and the hierarchy had gotten conservative. It was motivated mainly by protecting its own self-interests.

I might also point out that although the Black Muslim movement professed to be a religious group, the religion they had adopted—Islam—didn't recognize them. So religiously it was in a vacuum. And it didn't take part in politics, so it was not a political group. When you have an organization that's neither political nor religious and doesn't take part in the civil rights struggle, what can it call itself? It's in a vacuum. So all of these factors led to my splitting from the organization.

YOUNG SOCIALIST: What are the aims of your new organization?

MALCOLM X: There are two organizations. There's the Muslim Mosque, Inc., which is religious. Its aim is to create an atmosphere and facilities in which people who are interested in Islam can get a better understanding of Islam. The aim of the other organization, the Organization of Afro-American Unity, is to use whatever means necessary to bring about a society in which the twenty-two million Afro-Americans are recognized and respected as human beings.

YOUNG SOCIALIST: How do you define Black nationalism, with which you have been identified?

MALCOLM X: I used to define Black nationalism as the idea that the Black man should control the economy of his community, the politics of his community, and so forth.

But when I was in Africa in May, in Ghana, I was speaking with the Algerian ambassador who is extremely militant and is a revolutionary in the true sense of the word (and has his credentials as such for having carried on a successful revolution against oppression in his country). When I told him that my political, social, and economic philosophy was Black nationalism, he asked me very frankly: Well, where did that leave him? Because he was white. He was an African, but he was Algerian, and to all appearances, he was a white man. And he said if I define my objective as the victory of Black nationalism, where does that leave him? Where does that leave revolutionaries in Morocco, Egypt, Iraq, Mauritania? So he showed me where I was alienating people who were true revolutionaries dedicated to overturning the system of exploitation that exists on this earth by any means necessary.

So I had to do a lot of thinking and reappraising of my definition of Black nationalism. Can we sum up the solution to the problems confronting our people as Black nationalism? And if you notice, I haven't been using the expression for several months. But I still would be hard pressed to give a specific definition of the overall philosophy which I think is necessary for the liberation of the Black people in this country.

YOUNG SOCIALIST: Is it true, as is often said, that you favor violence?

MALCOLM X: I don't favor violence. If we could bring about recognition and respect of our people by peaceful means, well and good. Everybody would like to reach his objectives peacefully. But I'm also a realist. The only people in this country who are asked to be nonviolent are Black people. I've never heard anybody go to the Ku Klux Klan and teach them nonviolence, or to the [John] Birch Society and other right-wing elements. Nonviolence is only preached to Black Americans, and I don't go along with anyone who wants to teach our people nonviolence until someone at the same time is teaching our enemy to be nonviolent. I believe we should protect ourselves by any means necessary when we are attacked by racists.

YOUNG SOCIALIST: What do you think is responsible for race prejudice in the U.S.?

MALCOLM X: Ignorance and greed. And a skillfully designed program of miseducation that goes right along with the American system of exploitation and oppression.

If the entire American population were properly educated—by properly educated, I mean given a true picture of the history and contributions of the Black man—I think many whites would be less racist in their feelings. They would have more respect for the Black man as a human being. Knowing what the Black man's contributions to science and civilization have been in the past, the white man's feelings of superiority would be at least partially negated. Also, the feeling of inferiority that the Black man has would be replaced by a balanced knowledge of himself. He'd feel more like a human being. He'd function more like a human being, in a society of human beings.

So it takes education to eliminate it. And just because you have colleges and universities doesn't mean you have education. The colleges and universities in the American educational system are skillfully used to miseducate.

YOUNG SOCIALIST: What were the highlights of your trip to Africa?

MALCOLM X: I visited Egypt, Arabia, Kuwait, Lebanon, Sudan, Ethiopia, Kenya, Tanganyika, Zanzibar (now Tanzania), Nigeria, Ghana, Liberia, Guinea, and Algeria. During that trip I had audiences with President Nasser of Egypt, President Nyerere of Tanzania, President Jomo Kenyatta (who was then prime minister) of Kenya, Prime Minister Milton Obote of Uganda, President Azikiwe of Nigeria, President Nkrumah of Ghana, and President Sékou Touré of Guinea. I think the highlights were the audiences I had with those persons because it gave me a chance to sample their thinking. I was impressed by their analysis of the problem, and many of the suggestions they gave went a long way toward broadening my own outlook.

YOUNG SOCIALIST: How much influence does revolutionary Africa have on the thinking of Black people in this country?

MALCOLM X: All the influence in the world. You can't

separate the militancy that's displayed on the African continent from the militancy that's displayed right here among American Blacks. The positive image that is developing of Africans is also developing in the minds of Black Americans, and consequently they develop a more positive image of themselves. Then they take more positive steps—actions.

So you can't separate the African revolution from the mood of the Black man in America. Neither could the colonization of Africa be separated from the menial position that the Black man in this country was satisfied to stay in for so long. Since Africa has gotten its independence through revolution, you'll notice the stepped-up cry against discrimination that has appeared in the Black community.

YOUNG SOCIALIST: How do you view the role of the U.S. in the Congo?

MALCOLM X: As criminal. Probably there is no better example of criminal activity against an oppressed people than the role the U.S. has been playing in the Congo, through her ties with Tshombe and the mercenaries. You can't overlook the fact that Tshombe gets his money from the U.S. The money he uses to hire these mercenaries— these paid killers imported from South Africa—comes from the United States. The pilots that fly these planes have been trained by the U.S. The bombs themselves that are blowing apart the bodies of women and children come from the U.S. So I can only view the role of the United States in the Congo as a criminal role. And I think the seeds she is sowing in the Congo she will have to harvest. The chickens that she has turned loose over there have got to come home to roost.

YOUNG SOCIALIST: What about the U.S. role in South Vietnam?

MALCOLM X: The same thing. It shows the real ignorance of those who control the American power structure. If France, with all types of heavy arms, as deeply entrenched as she was in what then was called Indochina, couldn't stay there, I don't see how anybody in their right mind can think the U.S. can get in there—it's impossible. So it shows her ignorance, her blindness, her lack of foresight and hindsight; and her complete defeat in South Vietnam is only a matter of time.

YOUNG SOCIALIST: How do you view the activity of white and Black students who went to the South last summer and attempted to register Black people to vote?

MALCOLM X: The attempt was good—I should say the objective to register Black people in the South was good because the only real power a poor man in this country has is the power of the ballot. But I don't believe sending them in and telling them to be nonviolent was intelligent. I go along with the effort toward registration, but I think they should be permitted to use whatever means at their disposal to defend themselves from the attacks of the Klan, the White Citizens' Council, and other groups.

YOUNG SOCIALIST: What do you think of the murder of the three civil rights workers and what's happened to their killers?[32]

MALCOLM X: It shows that the society we live in is not actually what it tries to represent itself as to the rest of the world. This was murder and the federal government is helpless because the case involves Negroes. Even the whites involved, were involved in helping Negroes. And concerning anything in this society involved in helping Negroes, the federal government shows an inability to function. But it can function in South Vietnam, in the Congo, in Berlin,[33] and in other places where it has no business. But it can't function in Mississippi.

YOUNG SOCIALIST: In a recent speech you mentioned that you met John Lewis of SNCC in Africa.[34] Do you feel that the younger and more militant leaders in the South are broadening their views on the whole general struggle?

MALCOLM X: Sure. When I was in the Black Muslim movement I spoke on many white campuses and Black campuses. I knew back in 1961 and '62 that the younger generation was much different from the older, and that many students were more sincere in their analysis of the problem and their desire to see the problem solved. In foreign countries the students have helped bring about revolution—it was the students who brought about the revolution in the Sudan, who swept Syngman Rhee out of office in Korea, swept Menderes out in Turkey. The students didn't think in terms of the odds against them, and they couldn't be bought out.

In America students have been noted for involving themselves in panty raids, goldfish swallowing, seeing how many can get in a telephone booth—not for their revolutionary political ideas or their desire to change unjust conditions. But some students are becoming more like their brothers around the world. However, the students have been deceived somewhat in what's known as the civil rights struggle (which was never designed to solve the problem). The students were maneuvered in the direction of thinking the problem was already analyzed, so they didn't try to analyze it for themselves.

In my thinking, if the students in this country forgot the analysis that has been presented to them, and they went into a huddle and began to research this problem of racism for themselves, independent of politicians and independent of all the foundations (which are a part of the power structure), and did it themselves, then some of their findings would be shocking, but they would see that they would never be able to bring about a solution to racism in their country as long as they're relying on the government to do it.

The federal government itself is just as racist as the government in Mississippi, and is more guilty of perpetuating the racist system. At the federal level they are more shrewd, more skillful at doing it, just like the FBI is more skillful than the state police and the state police are more skillful than the local police.

The same with politicians. The politician at the federal level is usually more skilled than the politician at the local level, and when he wants to practice racism, he's more skilled in the practice of it than those who practice it at the local level.

YOUNG SOCIALIST: What is your opinion of the Democratic Party?

MALCOLM X: The Democratic Party is responsible for the racism that exists in this country, along with the Republican Party. The leading racists in this country are Democrats. Goldwater isn't the leading racist—he's a racist but not the leading racist.[35] The racists who have influence in Washington, D.C., are Democrats. If you check, whenever any kind of legislation is suggested to mitigate the injustices that Negroes suffer in this country, you will find that the people who line up against it are members of Lyndon B. Johnson's party. The Dixiecrats are Democrats. The Dixiecrats are only a subdivision of the Democratic Party, and the same man over the Democrats is over the Dixiecrats.[36]

YOUNG SOCIALIST: What contribution can youth, especially students, who are disgusted with racism in this society, make to the Black struggle for freedom?

MALCOLM X: Whites who are sincere don't accomplish anything by joining Negro organizations and making them integrated. Whites who are sincere should organize among themselves and figure out some strategy to break down the prejudice that exists in white communities. This is where they can function more intelligently and more effectively, in the white community itself, and this has never been done.

YOUNG SOCIALIST: What part in the world revolution are youth playing, and what lessons may this have for American youth?

MALCOLM X: If you've studied the captives being caught by the American soldiers in South Vietnam, you'll find that these guerrillas are young people. Some of them are just children and some haven't yet reached their teens. Most are teenagers. It is the teenagers abroad, all over the world, who are actually involving themselves in the struggle to eliminate oppression and exploitation. In the

Congo, the refugees point out that many of the Congolese revolutionaries are children. In fact, when they shoot captive revolutionaries, they shoot all the way down to seven years old—that's been reported in the press. Because the revolutionaries are children, young people. In these countries the young people are the ones who most quickly identify with the struggle and the necessity to eliminate the evil conditions that exist. And here in this country, it has been my own observation that when you get into a conversation on racism and discrimination and segregation, you will find young people are more incensed over it—they feel more filled with an urge to eliminate it.

I think young people here can find a powerful example in the young *simbas* [lions] in the Congo and the young fighters in South Vietnam.

Another point: as the dark-skinned nations of this earth become independent, as they develop and become stronger, that means that time is on the side of the American Negro. At this point the American Negro is still hospitable and friendly and forgiving. But if he is continually tricked and deceived and so on, and if there is still no solution to his problems, he will become completely disillusioned, disenchanted, and disassociate himself from the interest of America and its society. Many have done that already.

YOUNG SOCIALIST: What is your opinion of the worldwide struggle now going on between capitalism and socialism?

MALCOLM X: It is impossible for capitalism to survive, primarily because the system of capitalism needs some blood to suck. Capitalism used to be like an eagle, but now it's more like a vulture. It used to be strong enough to go and suck anybody's blood whether they were strong or not. But now it has become more cowardly, like the vulture, and it can only suck the blood of the helpless. As the nations of the world free themselves, then capitalism has less victims, less to suck, and it becomes weaker and weaker. It's only a matter of time in my opinion before it will collapse completely.

YOUNG SOCIALIST: What is the outlook for the Negro struggle in 1965?

MALCOLM X: Bloody. It was bloody in 1963, it was bloody in 1964, and all of the causes that created this bloodshed still remain. The March on Washington was designed to serve as a vent or valve for the frustration that produced this explosive atmosphere.[37] In 1964 they used the civil rights bill as a valve. What can they use in 1965? There is no trick that the politicians can use to contain the explosiveness that exists right here in Harlem.

And look at New York Police Commissioner Murphy. He's coming out in headlines trying to make it a crime now to even predict that there's going to be trouble.[38] This shows the caliber of American thinking. There's going to be an explosion, but don't talk about it. All the ingredients that produce explosions exist, but don't talk about it, he says. That's like saying 700 million Chinese don't exist.[39] This is the same approach. The American has become so guilt-ridden and filled with fear that instead of facing the reality of any situation, he pretends the situation doesn't exist. You know, in this country it's almost a crime to say there's a place called China—unless you mean that little island called Formosa. By the same token, it's almost a crime to say that people in Harlem are going to explode because the social dynamite that existed last year is still here.

So I think 1965 will be most explosive—more explosive than it was in '64 and '63. There's nothing they can do to contain it. The Negro leaders have lost their control over the people. So that when the people begin to explode— and their explosion is justified, not unjustified—the Negro leaders can't contain it.

An authentic voice of the forces of the American revolution

IN TRIBUTE TO MALCOLM X, BY JACK BARNES, MARCH 5, 1965

The following are excerpts from a speech given by Jack Barnes at a memorial meeting for Malcolm X organized by the Militant Labor Forum in New York. Other speakers included James Shabazz of the Muslim Mosque, Inc.; Robert Vernon, a writer for the *Militant;* and Farrell Dobbs, national secretary of the Socialist Workers Party. The meeting was chaired by 1964 SWP presidential candidate Clifton DeBerry.

I would like to speak tonight not only for the socialist youth of the Young Socialist Alliance, but also for the young revolutionists in our movement around the world who would want to speak at a memorial for Malcolm X but who cannot be here. This is especially true of those in Africa, the Middle East, France, and England, who recently had a chance to see and hear Malcolm.

Malcolm was the leader of the struggle for Black liberation. He was, as stated at his funeral by Ossie Davis, the Black shining prince, the manhood of the Harlems of the world.[40] To his people he first and foremost belongs.

But he was also the teacher, inspirer, and leader of a much smaller group, the revolutionary socialist youth of America. He was to us the face and the authentic voice of the forces of the American revolution. And above all, he spoke the truth for our generation of revolutionists.

What attracted revolutionary youth to Malcolm X? More important, what often made youth—including white youth—who listened to him revolutionists? I think there were two main things. First, he spoke the simple truth—unadorned, unvarnished, and uncompromising. Second was the evolution and content of Malcolm's political thought.

Malcolm saw the depth of the hypocrisy and falsehood that covers the real social relations in American society. To him the key was not so much the lies that the ruling class and its spokesmen propagated, but the lies and the falsehoods about his people—their past and their potentialities—which they accepted.

Malcolm's message to the ghetto, his agitation against racism, was a special kind. What he had to say and what he did stemmed from a study of the history of the Afro-Americans. He explained that in order for Black Americans to know what to do—to know how to go about winning freedom—they had to first answer three questions: Where did you come from? How did you get here? Who is responsible for your condition?

Malcolm's truth was so explosive because it stemmed from a careful study of how the Afro-American was enslaved and dehumanized. He publicized the facts that have been suppressed from the regular history books and kept out of the schools.

While in the Black Muslims and after he left, Malcolm taught that the process by which the Africans were made into slaves was one of dehumanizing them. Through barbarous cruelty, comparable to the worst Nazi concentration camps, they were taught to fear the white man. They were systematically stripped of their language, culture, history, names, religion, of all connections with their home in Africa—of their identity. They were named *Negro,* signifying this lack of identity and this denial of their African origin.

Especially after their "emancipation" they were taught the Christianity of meekness and submission and of their reward in heaven. They were taught that Africa was a jungle where people lived in mud huts, and that the white man had done them a great favor in bringing them to America.

Malcolm asked the Black American: Who taught you to hate yourself? Who taught you to be a pacifist? Was *he* a pacifist? Who said Black people cannot defend themselves? Does *he* defend himself? Who taught you not to go too far and too fast in your fight for freedom? Did *he* stand to lose something by the speed of your victory? Who taught you to vote for the fox to escape the wolf? What does the fox give you in return?

All these questions, and so many more, needed no answers. All the questions were directed to those who had nothing to lose and no stake in the system as it exists now.

His political thought was the other important factor in the development of those who were taught by him. First, he believed in and explained the need for Afro-American unity. He felt it was necessary to base your alliances on your own unity, and reject unconditionally any degrading or compromising alliances. It is only upon the basis of this unity, and the dignity and self-respect that goes along with it, that the battle for freedom can be waged. Those who would bypass this step would condemn the Black Americans to be a tail to the kite of other, more conservative forces.

"We cannot think of uniting with others, until after we have first united among ourselves. We cannot think of being acceptable to others until we have first proven acceptable to ourselves. One can't unite bananas with scattered leaves."[41] Malcolm knew that Afro-Americans had enough of this kind of unity—with the liberals, the Communist Party, and the Socialist Party.

Secondly, he spoke of self-defense, and the real meaning of violence. He continually pointed out that the source of violence was the oppressor, not the oppressed. He continually pointed to the use of violence by the oppressor. Out of one side of its mouth the government and press preach pacifism to the American Negro, while out of the other side comes the cold announcement that they will destroy as many North Vietnamese as they wish. Malcolm never

tired of pointing out the hypocrisy of this form of pacifism, its ineffectuality and its degrading and masochistic
character.

Malcolm told us, at the first Militant Labor Forum at
which he spoke, that "if George Washington didn't get
independence for this country nonviolently, and if Patrick
Henry didn't come up with a nonviolent statement, and
you taught me to look upon them as patriots and heroes,
then it's time for you to realize that I have studied your
books well. . . . No white person would go about fighting
for freedom in the same manner that he has helped me
and you to fight for our freedom. No, none of them would.
When it comes to Black freedom, then the white man
freedom-rides and sits in, he's nonviolent, he sings, 'We
Shall Overcome,' and all that stuff. But when the property of the white man is threatened, or the freedom of the
white man is threatened, he's not nonviolent."[42]

Thirdly, unlike any other Black leader, and unlike any
other mass leader in my lifetime, he continually exposed
the real role of the Democratic Party, and pointed to the
mistake in believing the federal government of this country would free the Afro-American. He said, "The Democrats get Negro support, yet the Negroes get nothing in
return. The Negroes put the Democrats first, yet the
Democrats put the Negroes last. And the alibi that the
Democrats use—they blame the Dixiecrats. A Dixiecrat is
nothing but a Democrat in disguise. . . . Because Dixie in
reality means all that territory south of the Canadian
border."[43]

Malcolm X always sought to expose those who were
really responsible for maintaining the racism of this society rather than directing his fire at the puppets. When
New York Police Commissioner Murphy attacked him
and others as "irresponsible," Malcolm responded that
Murphy was only doing his job. Mayor Wagner, Murphy's
boss, was the one responsible for the charge, he said.

Malcolm never tired of explaining and demonstrating
that it was the federal government headed by President

Johnson that was responsible for maintaining racism in the North and South. In doing this he showed the continuity of the inhuman treatment of Negroes and the responsibility of those who run this society for the condition of the Black people. As one of his followers, Benjamin, pointed out at a meeting of the Organization of Afro-American Unity, the North is responsible for the racism in the South, because "they won the Civil War."

It was in talking about the Democratic Party that another aspect of Malcolm came clearly to the fore. This was his ability to translate the complicated and important ideas which he developed and absorbed into the language of those he knew would change the world. The ability to speak clearly to the oppressed has been the unique genius of all great revolutionary leaders in history.

The [June 1, 1964] *Militant* reported that Malcolm, at his press conference, spoke of President Johnson as being hypocritical. He pointed out that LBJ's closest friend in the Senate, Richard Russell, was leading the fight against the civil rights bill. Malcolm was challenged by a reporter who doubted that Johnson's friendship with Russell proved anything. Malcolm looked at him with his usual smile and said, off the cuff, "If you tell me you're against robbing banks and your best friend is Jesse James, I have grounds to doubt your sincerity."

The final point in his political development that was so important for the education of those young people who followed him, looked to him, and in many ways were educated by him, was his revolutionary internationalism.

Malcolm gave at least three reasons for his international outlook. First was the common identity of the power structure which practiced racism in this country and which practiced imperialism abroad. "This system is not only ruling us in America, it is ruling the world," he said.

Second, only through Afro-Americans realizing that they were part of a great majority of nonwhites in the world who were fighting for and winning freedom would they have the courage to fight the battle for freedom with whatever means necessary.

Malcolm said that "among the so-called Negroes in this country, as a rule the civil rights groups, those who believe in civil rights, they spend most of their time trying to prove they are Americans. Their thinking is usually domestic, confined to the boundaries of America, and they always look upon themselves . . . upon the American stage, the American stage is a white stage. So a Black man standing on that stage in America automatically is in the minority. He is the underdog, and in his struggle he always uses an approach that is a begging, hat-in-hand, compromising approach." But, he said: We don't beg, we don't thank you for giving us what you should have given us a hundred years ago.[44]

Last, was the fact that in the final analysis freedom could only be won in one place when it was won everywhere. In Africa, he said, "Our problem is your problem. . . . Your problems will never be fully solved until and unless ours are solved. You will never be fully respected until and unless we are also respected. You will never be recognized as free human beings until and unless we are also recognized and treated as human beings."[45]

Though Malcolm X came from the American ghetto, spoke for the American ghetto, and directed his message to the American ghetto first of all, he is a figure of world importance, and developed his ideas in relation to the great events of world history in his time.

If Malcolm X is to be compared with any international figure, the most striking parallel is with Fidel Castro. Both of them belong to the generation that was shaped ideologically under the twin circumstances of World War II and the monstrous betrayals and defaults of the Stalinized Communist parties. These men found their way independently to the revolutionary struggle, bypassing both Social Democracy and Stalinism.

Each started from the struggle of his own oppressed people for liberation. Each embraced the nationalism of his people as necessary to mobilize them to struggle for their freedom. Each stressed the importance of the solidarity of the oppressed all over the world in their struggle against a common oppressor.

Fidel did not start out as a thoroughgoing Marxist or as a revolutionary socialist. Like Malcolm, he was determined to pursue the national liberation of his people by "whatever means necessary" and without any compromises with those with any stake in the status quo.

Fidel Castro's dedication to political independence and to economic development for Cuba led him eventually to opposition to capitalism. So, also, Malcolm's uncompromising stand against racism brought him to identify with the revolutions of the colonial people who were turning against capitalism, and finally to conclude that the elimination of capitalism in this country was necessary for freedom. Just as Fidel Castro discovered that there can be no political independence and economic development in a colonial country without breaking from capitalism, so Malcolm had come to the conclusion that capitalism and racism were so entangled in the United States that you had to uproot the system in order to eliminate racism.

Malcolm's Black nationalism was aimed at preparing Black people to struggle for their freedom. "The greatest mistake of the movement," he said in an interview in the February 25 *Village Voice,* "has been trying to organize a sleeping people around specific goals. You have to wake the people up first, then you'll get action."

"Wake them up to their exploitation?" the interviewer asked.

"No, to their humanity, to their own worth, and to their heritage," he answered.

Everything he said to the Black people was designed to raise their confidence, to organize them independently of those who oppressed them, to teach them who was responsible for their condition and who their allies were. He explained that they were part of the great majority—the nonwhites and the oppressed of the world. He taught that freedom could be won only by fighting for it; it has never been given to anyone. He explained that it could be won only by making a real revolution that uproots and changes the entire society.

Thus it is not surprising that many who considered themselves socialists, radicals, and even Marxists could not recognize and identify with Malcolm's revolutionary character. They could not recognize the revolutionary content of this great leader clothed in the new forms, language, and dark colors of the American proletarian ghetto.

Even with all his uniqueness and greatness as an individual, he could not have reached this understanding unless the conditions in this country were such that it was possible. Even though no one can fill his shoes, the fact that he did what he did, developed as the revolutionary leader he was, is the proof of more Malcolms to come.

He was a proof as Fidel was a proof. Fidel stood up ninety miles away from the most powerful imperialism in the world and thumbed his nose and showed us, "See, it can be done. They can't go on controlling the world forever."

Malcolm went even further than Fidel, because Malcolm challenged American capitalism from right inside. He was the living proof for our generation of revolutionists that it can and will happen here.

Our job, the job of the YSA, is to teach the revolutionary youth of this country to tell the difference between the nationalism of the oppressed and the nationalism of the oppressor, to teach them to differentiate the forces of liberation from the forces of the exploiters; to teach them to hear the voices of the revolution regardless of the forms they take; to teach them to differentiate between the self-defense of the victim and violence of the aggressor; to teach them to refuse to give an inch to white liberalism and to reach out to Malcolm's heirs, the vanguard of the ghetto, as brothers and comrades.

1. An account of Malcolm X's trip to Ghana can be found in *The Autobiography of Malcolm X* (New York: Ballantine, 1973), pp. 352-60.

2. Angola was then a colony of Portugal; it won its independence in 1975.

3. The most well-known victim of this practice was the singer Paul Robeson. Another important case was that of Black journalist William Worthy, who had to fight a two-year legal battle to overturn a 1962 conviction for visiting Cuba after he had been denied a passport.

4. In May 1964 New York's daily newspapers ran lurid stories alleging the existence of a gang of young Blacks, calling themselves "Blood Brothers," that had supposedly been organized by dissident Black Muslims to attack whites. For the talk on this subject given by Malcolm X on his return to the United States, see *Malcolm X Speaks,* pp. 64-71.

5. On April 7, 1964, Rev. Bruce Klunder was crushed to death by a bulldozer during a civil rights demonstration at a school construction site in Cleveland.

6. The Civil Rights Act of 1964, signed into law by Pres. Lyndon B. Johnson on July 2, banned discrimination in voting, public facilities, schools, and employment. Two weeks earlier, three civil rights workers—two white, one Black—had disappeared in Philadelphia, Mississippi. The battered bodies of Michael Schwerner, Andrew Goodman, and James E. Chaney were found on August 4. At the time of the Oxford Union debate the FBI had still made no arrests.

7. Ruling on a case called *Brown v. Board of Education,* the U.S. Supreme Court declared in 1954 that segregated school systems, which it had previously upheld as lawful, were in violation of the Constitution.

8. On July 16, 1964, a fifteen-year-old Black youth, James Powell, was shot and killed by a New York police officer. Two days later, a demonstration at a central Harlem police station demanding the officer's arrest was broken up by police, and the organizers were arrested. Police then raged through the area, beating, arresting, and shooting residents, killing one. The

ensuing rebellion in Harlem and the predominantly Black community of Bedford-Stuyvesant in Brooklyn lasted five days.

9. Four days before Malcolm X spoke, President Johnson announced a massive escalation of the war against Vietnam, including sustained bombing of North Vietnam and a big increase in U.S. combat troops. By the end of July, there were 75,000 U.S. troops in Vietnam.

10. In 1954 the French army suffered a decisive defeat at the hands of Vietnamese liberation forces at Dien Bien Phu. The U.S. government moved in, however, to replace France as the dominant imperialist power in the region, propping up a subservient regime in South Vietnam.

11. Ian Smith was the prime minister of the white-minority regime administering the British colony of Southern Rhodesia.

12. In April 1955 representatives of twenty-nine countries of Africa and Asia met in Bandung, Indonesia. The conference approved a final communiqué opposing "racial segregation and discrimination . . . in large regions of Africa and in other parts of the world," and declaring colonialism "an evil which should speedily be brought to an end."

13. The December 31, 1962, issue of *Look* details four days of secret negotiations in late September of that year to arrange a staged confrontation in which Gov. Ross Barnett was to be seen blocking Meredith from entering the university to register. Barnett would then step aside when federal marshals drew their guns. The deal fell through, however. Barnett proved unable to control racist mobs he had helped mobilize, and President Kennedy was forced to send in 2,500 federal troops to establish control.

14. The Emancipation Proclamation went into effect January 1, 1863, freeing slaves in the Southern states that were in rebellion against the federal government in the U.S. Civil War.

15. Medgar Evers, a leader of the National Association for the Advancement of Colored People (NAACP) in Mississippi, was assassinated by racist gunmen in front of his home on June 12, 1963. On Sunday morning, September 15, 1963, a bomb exploded in Birmingham, Alabama, in the Sixteenth Street Baptist Church, which had been the staging point for desegregation demonstrations. Four young Black people were killed by

the bomb and about twenty were injured.

16. The Great Society was the theme of President Johnson's January 1965 State of the Union speech to Congress.

17. Previously published excerpts of this speech gave its date as December 31, 1964. In his talk, however, Malcolm X identifies the day as Friday, that is, January 1, 1965.

18. White Citizens' Councils were racist organizations that developed in the South in the mid-1950s to oppose moves to desegregate education and other public facilities.

19. The Big Six was a term used by the mass media to refer to a number of the most prominent figures in the civil rights movement. These were A. Philip Randolph, then a vice president of the American Federation of Labor–Congress of Industrial Organizations (AFL-CIO); Martin Luther King, Jr., of the Southern Christian Leadership Conference (SCLC); Roy Wilkins of the NAACP; James Farmer of the Congress of Racial Equality (CORE); Whitney Young of the Urban League; and Bayard Rustin, a main organizer of the 1963 March on Washington.

20. Hideki Tojo was prime minister of Japan during most of World War II.

21. On August 8, 1963, Mao Zedong, chairman of the Communist Party of China, made a statement calling on "persons of all colors in the world . . . to unite against the racial discrimination practiced by U.S. imperialism and to support American Negroes in their struggle against racial discrimination."

22. The Mississippi Freedom Democratic Party, formed in April 1964, had tried without success at the Democrats' August 1964 national convention to obtain the ouster of delegates from Mississippi's segregationist Democratic organization. The MFDP then announced its own candidates for the November voting and conducted a Freedom Election open to all Mississippi residents, registered or not. After the elections, Fannie Lou Hamer toured the North as part of an MFDP team that denounced the exclusion of Blacks from the official Mississippi voting and called on Congress not to seat those elected. Malcolm X's speech to the December 20, 1964, rally in Harlem in support of the MFDP is printed in *Malcolm X Speaks,* pp. 105-14.

23. On January 4, 1965, the U.S. Congress was to begin a new session. Many civil rights and other organizations were supporting the MFDP demand that Congress refuse to seat the winners in the elections in Mississippi, from which Black voters had been excluded.

24. The founding program of the Organization of Afro-American Unity, dated June 28, 1964, can be found, together with an OAAU statement of February 15, 1965, in George Breitman, *The Last Year of Malcolm X: The Evolution of a Revolutionary* (New York: Pathfinder, 1967), pp. 105-24.

25. COFO was the Council of Federated Organizations, a coalition of civil rights groups in Mississippi formed in 1961.

26. Malcolm X is referring to the Black Muslim leadership's response to an attack against its members by Los Angeles police in 1962. On April 27 of that year, police shot seven unarmed Black Muslims, killing one and crippling another for life. They then arrested sixteen of their victims on false charges of assaulting the police. Malcolm X organized a broad defense campaign involving many Black community organizations in Los Angeles. As he was preparing to launch the campaign on a national scale, the Chicago headquarters of the Nation of Islam called off the entire effort, restricting defense work to the courts. This episode is described in Breitman, *The Last Year of Malcolm X,* pp. 15-19.

27. Mau Mau was the name given to rebel groups that carried out an armed struggle during the 1950s against British colonial rule in Kenya. The British authorities jailed Kenyatta in 1953 as a leader of that struggle.

28. Tshombe was in exile in Europe in 1963-64.

29. Manhattan congressman William Fitts Ryan announced December 23, 1964, that he would introduce a resolution to deny seats in the House of Representatives to the five candidates declared elected in the official voting the previous month. Harlem congressman Adam Clayton Powell was one of sixteen other representatives supporting the resolution.

30. Malcolm X spoke in Alabama February 3 and 4. He was scheduled to speak in Mississippi later that month but was assassinated before he could make the trip.

31. In a February 15, 1965, speech in New York, Malcolm X

said of Elijah Muhammad, "Yes, he's immoral. You can't take nine teenaged women and seduce them and give them babies . . . and then tell me you're moral." See *Malcolm X: The Last Speeches* (New York: Pathfinder, 1989), pp. 121-22.

32. In early December 1964, more than five months after the murder of the three civil rights workers in Mississippi, the FBI arrested twenty-one men. Charges were dismissed the following week because of "insufficient evidence." After three years of delay, seven were eventually convicted and sentenced to prison terms ranging from three to ten years.

33. During the 1960s, the United States maintained a garrison of more than five thousand troops in Berlin. In October 1961 U.S. and Soviet tanks had faced each other in a standoff across the newly built Berlin Wall in the heart of the occupied city.

34. Malcolm X spoke of his meeting with John Lewis at a January 7, 1965, meeting of the Militant Labor Forum. See *Malcolm X Speaks,* p. 209. Some comments by Lewis and another SNCC leader on the impact in Africa of Malcolm X's trip there can be found in *Malcolm X Speaks,* p. 85.

35. In the 1964 presidential election, the Republican candidate Barry Goldwater, who had made open appeals to racist and extreme anticommunist sentiment, was defeated by the Democratic candidate, Johnson.

36. The Dixiecrats were the openly segregationist and racist wing of the Democratic Party dominant at the time in most of the U.S. South.

37. The August 28, 1963, March on Washington drew more than 250,000 people for a rally at the Lincoln Memorial. The march called for passage of civil rights legislation then pending in Congress.

38. On January 10, 1965, New York Police Commissioner Michael J. Murphy sharply criticized Black leaders such as Malcolm X who had pointed to the mood of frustration in the Black ghettos and had predicted future outbreaks of resistance. It was such warnings, Murphy implied, that were causing the trouble.

39. Until the early 1970s, the U.S. government refused to recognize the People's Republic of China, maintaining instead

that the right-wing government on Taiwan (Formosa) represented China.

40. Ossie Davis's eulogy is printed in John Henrik Clarke,
Malcolm X: The Man and His Times (Trenton, N.J.: Africa
World Press, 1990), pp. xi-xii.

41. *Malcolm X Speaks,* p. 22. From Malcolm X's March 12,
1964, press statement announcing he was leaving the Nation of
Islam and forming the Muslim Mosque, Inc.

42. *Two Speeches by Malcolm X* (New York: Pathfinder,
1987), p. 11, and *By Any Means Necessary,* p. 22. *Two Speeches
by Malcolm X* contains the full text of Malcolm's talk. For the
question period, see *By Any Means Necessary,* pp. 14-32.

43. *Two Speeches by Malcolm X,* p. 18.

44. *Two Speeches by Malcolm X,* pp. 14-15.

45. *Malcolm X Speaks,* pp. 74-75. From a memorandum sub-
mitted by Malcolm X to the July 17-21, 1964, meeting of the
Organization of African Unity in Cairo, Egypt.

Other titles from Pathfinder

U.S. Hands Off the Mideast!
Cuba Speaks Out at the United Nations
by Fidel Castro and Ricardo Alarcón, $9.95

Blacks in America's Wars
by Robert Mullen, $7.95

Cointelpro: The FBI's Secret War on Political Freedom
by Nelson Blackstock, $14.95

Fighting Racism in World War II
by George Breitman, et al., $19.95

The Changing Face of U.S. Politics
The Proletarian Party and the Trade Unions
edited by Jack Barnes, $18.95

Out Now!
*A Participant's Account of the Movement in
the U.S. against the Vietnam War*
by Fred Halstead, $29.95

Nelson Mandela: The Struggle Is My Life
by Nelson Mandela, $12.95

Nelson Mandela: Speeches 1990
'Intensify the Struggle to Abolish Apartheid'
by Nelson Mandela, $5.00

Thomas Sankara Speaks
The Burkina Faso Revolution 1983-87, $17.95

Che Guevara and the Cuban Revolution
Writings and Speeches of Ernesto Che Guevara, $20.95

In Defense of Socialism
by Fidel Castro, $12.95

The Communist Manifesto
by Karl Marx and Frederick Engels, $2.50

Cosmetics, Fashions, and the Exploitation of Women
by Joseph Hansen and Evelyn Reed
introduction by Mary-Alice Waters, $11.95

Teamster Bureaucracy
The Trade Union Campaign against World War II
by Farrell Dobbs, $17.95

Write for a free catalog.